Praise for *Real Li*

"A breakthrough in how to have a "............ .... with God; this book is a tremendous example of living with the Holy Spirit's power in your life."

- Chris Widener, author of The Art of Influence
and The Leadership Rules www.ChrisWidener.com

"Real Life is really simple; simple practical truths, principles and precepts born out of a love relationship with God that spills over into every other area. Love, integrity, passion, loyalty, compassion, success, and honor are some of the qualities emergent from our relationship with God. Robyn has captured these and expresses them so simply that all of us can grasp them. These thoughts, meditations will help frame your day."

- Barbara J. Yoder, Senior Pastor and Lead Apostle, Shekinah
www.shekinahchurch.org; www.barbarayoderblog.com

"Robyn writes in a down to earth, relatable; and easy to read manner. These devotions are inspiring, as they provide a quick and timely reminder of God's truth that will bring life and encouragement to your day."

- Pastor Neil Kelly, lead pastor of The Rock - Kalamazoo
www.gototherock.com

"Fresh wholesome fruit! "Real Life" captures real life events and applies Biblical truths to those events. Look through Robyn's eyes as a preacher's kid, mother, and successful entrepreneur as she 'opens' your own eyes in your daily walk."

- Jon Mark Hott, Mark Hott Ministries, 3 John 2

ROBYN WILSON

FREEDOM AND HOPE, LLC

PAW PAW, MI

Real Life...with a Real God
Wilson, Robyn
Published by: Freedom and Hope, LLC Paw Paw, MI

Scriptures taken from the Holy Bible, New International Version®, NIV®. Copyright ©
1973, 1978, 1984, 2011 by Biblica, Inc.™ Used by permission of Zondervan. All rights
reserved worldwide. www.zondervan.com The "NIV" and "New International Version" are trademarks registered in the United States Patent and Trademark Office by
Biblica, Inc.™

First Edition, Published 2013

Printed in the United States of America

Cover Art Design: Jennifer Phillips
Editor and Interior Design & Layout: Jennifer Du Charme

ISBN-10: 0989476308
ISBN-13: 978-0-9894763-0-0

I dedicate this book to
My precious girls:
Darienne, Lindsey & Madison
Babies, this has been a long couple years,
and you are the reason I chose to keep going

Priscilla, thank you for coming alongside me
in such a special way

Jen, without you, this project
wouldn't have come together

Much love to you all
~Robyn

Contents

Foreward

"Give us this day our daily bread" is a recognized line from the Lord's Prayer where we ask God to provide us with our food on a daily basis. He always comes through. We eat every day and we rarely, if ever, have to go searching for food. We make our own meals, share meals with friends at work and get invited to dine with friends, family and colleagues.

Like our food choices, God has provided us with a multitude of ways to feed our souls. The obvious place to feed our soul is the Bible. Children's laughter, a painting that inspires us, a sculpture that speaks volumes through the unspoken word, a glance from a loved one, a neck-squeezing hug from a toddler, a baby grabbing your finger and never letting go are a few ways that God can say, "I love you", and nourish our inner selves.

God also fills our souls with cartoons that make us smile, novels that allow us to feel joy as the authors pen tales of sacrifice and hardship that inspire us to want to do more, be more and serve more.

God also gave us this book - Real Life With a Real God - and its author, the loving, talented and caring Robyn Wilson. Like the Lord's Prayer asking for our daily bread, this book gives us a daily shot of hope, faith and clarity by taking everyday life situations and relating them in a way that educate and inspire us.

When you invest your time in this book you get an immediate pay-back. You will gain an understanding of yourself and how God helps you through life - sometimes holding your hand, sometimes running beside you, lifting the training wheels and letting you go so you can find your balance and step into your next level of greatness.

Robyn shows us how God helps us celebrate ourselves and our gifts and talents to the highest level so we can make our marks on this earth, make a difference in people's lives and live our life closer to God.

May you be blessed by the contents of this book and its author, as I am.

Barry Spilchuk
Author - THE cANCER DANCE
Coauthor - A Cup of Chicken Soup for the Soul®
www.THEcancerDANCE.com

P.S.: Like the cover of this book suggests, proceed with caution because you will read the truth, the whole truth and nothing but the truth from this fun and stimulating author. The CAUTION tape was used to save her from making this book 900 pages long...stay tuned for her next God-inspired book...

Introduction

This book has been a compilation over time. God has brought me closer to Him through a variety of means, from direct revelation in our personal time, my healings, words spoken over me and written- both in the Bible and by others. My desire is to live to the fullness of the destiny for which He created me. As Psalm 105:1 says, "Give thanks to the Lord, call on His Name; make known among the nations what He has done." And that's what I want to do in this book~ begin to share with you some of what He has done in and for me, the likes of which He can also do in and through you! You're not here by accident, nor did you pick up this book by mistake. Let God use it to continue you on your personal journey deeper into Him! God loves you, and so do I!

Blessings all over you! ~Robyn

My Life is Like a Juicer!

Blessed are those who hunger and thirst for righteous-
ness, for they shall be filled. (Matthew 5:6)

O Lord, we have waited for you: the desire of our soul is for
Your Name and for the remembrance of You. (Isaiah 26:8b)

My life is like a juicer! At first glance, that sentence may not make much sense to you, but go with me on this for a few moments...

My folks got us an awesome juicer for Christmas. It's one of the best gifts we've gotten and we use it almost every day. When our girls get up in the mornings, they each peel an orange, because I generally have their carrot, celery and apple ready to go by the time they hit the kitchen. Sometimes we add grapes, and I add other veggies, but that's the basic flavor profile we use. As we add the whole food into the top of the machine, it spins on the inside and juice comes flowing out into the cup. Voila! A fresh drink to strengthen and sustain our bodies throughout the day. How much this parallels with our spiritual lives! We read our Bibles, worship God, pray, hear a message, the Holy Spirit spins it into our spirits, and voila! We have strength for the tasks ahead!

We need to realize, though, that not all fruits and veggies produce the same amount of juice~ in fact some produce none at all. You can never stick a banana into a juicer! A grape gives one small spurt of juice, while a pineapple, despite its size, yields only a fraction of the juice squeezed from a much smaller cucumber. I don't know all the tasks that lie ahead of me each day, but I know I want to be prepared, which is why I take in the juice regularly. Making fresh juice once a month or even once a week wouldn't provide me with the same health benefits that I get from drinking it five days a week: it's just good for my body, and the benefits compound as I keep drinking it.

Continue the parallel: I spend my time with God in praise, worship, Bible, hearing a message, and prayer, and I'm prepared for whatever the day may hold, well-filled in my spirit, which sustains me. My relationship with Him builds, compounds, over time. I discern His voice more easily, see deeper truth nuggets in the Word, become more whole, more like Him and less damaged by the world. Sometimes I think I'm busy and don't get more than a handful of "grapes", but other days I focus in, keep my priorities right, and fill up with juicy "cucumbers and oranges"! How much more strength I have those days!

God asks for our all, our best, every day. We are His Body in this world. Different tasks demand different priority or intensity: supporting a friend at a funeral is a different level of intensity than playing a game with one of my girls, and different also than strategizing a game plan with a business teammate to keep their house or keep their marriage together. Sure, I could get by with a 'grape-sized' amount of God-time if I'm hanging out and playing games, but who's on the other end of the phone when it rings? Am I prepared for the task ahead? Will that person get my best, and will I please God with my response? If my spirit is dry because I haven't 'made any juice' today~ spent any time with Him, what of true value do I have to give? Even if it is a day to play games with my girls, don't they, of all people, deserve the very best "me" I can give, filled to the brim with God, instead of just enough of Him to "get by"?

Dear Father, I long to drink in Your Spirit so I can exhale Your love to this world You've placed me in and this sphere of influence You've entrusted me with! My soul is thirsty for connection with You! Fill me with Your Spirit as I meet with You, so I'm not dry in my soul, but honor You instead.

In Jesus' Name, Amen

Take the Trade!

*Therefore, if anyone is in Christ, he is a new creation; the
old has gone, the new has come! (2 Corinthians 5:17)*

*You were taught, with regard to your former way of life to put off your
old self, which is being corrupted by its deceitful desires; to be made
now in the attitude of your minds; and to put on the new self created
to be like God in true righteousness and holiness. (Ephesians 4:22-24)*

Happy New Year! Now that we're almost two weeks into it, how are
you doing in writing the new digits in your checkbook register? I'm still
getting used to it too~ a simple change, but a change nonetheless.

Did you know God is into change? It's one of His specialties! He has
this really cool way of totally loving us, I mean being universally mad
about us just as we are, and yet at the same time His powerful love doesn't
allow Him to leave us in the mess we're in when He finds us.

If you're already in relationship with Him, think about where you
were in life when you met Him. Is that a place you miss, or wanted to stay?
Me neither. If you're exploring the idea of knowing Him in a personal way,
let me encourage you: if you seek peace~ He's got it. If you want love~
that's His essence. If you want guidance~ He's the Wonderful Counselor.

The Bible goes on and on with the attributes He has that He's willing to trade out for what you have: brokenness, confusion, anger, poverty. He has~ and is~ the answer to all that and so much more!

The best news about this exchange is that He doesn't require you to change before He gives you the trade. He comes alongside, right into the muck you feel like you're stuck in, and lifts you up, cleans you off, and patches you up. All of us are "in progress", becoming more like Him with each right choice we make. Ultimately His goal is that you enter a relationship with Him and allow Him to work with you at your own pace, restoring you to the destiny He created you for. He doesn't want to leave you in just the "patched up" state; He wants you completely whole! How's that for a change? Hence the term of Christianity being the "Good News"!

Dear Father, Thank You for coming alongside me in my mess and gently picking me up, cleaning me off, and giving me hope for the new year. Thank you that change isn't scary when I know Your heart for me is good and loving. Thank You that You never give up on me, no matter what!

In Jesus' Name, Amen

Ice Fishing Footsteps

"Come follow Me", Jesus said. (Matthew 3:19a)

A story from the past…

My former husband went out ice fishing with a buddy. They were the first ones on the lake this season, which is unusual for him~ generally he waits until there have been several other guys out before he ventures. Our lake is beautiful, but because it's spring-fed, it doesn't freeze evenly, and soft spots can make the journey from shore to fishing hole treacherous! It's no fun to go through the ice at 20 degrees air temp...

He could have easily exited out of our house through the garage, trekked down the hill and out onto the ice- it would have been shorter, but not wise. Instead he chose to drive around to the other side of the lake and follow the same path that had been successful for his buddy~ his buddy who knew the location of the springs, and already sat on his bucket, waiting, lantern burning brightly, clearly visible from our home. Later that morning he returned, happy they had both "limited out" on the fish. He also had a safe path from his ice fishing hole directly to our shoreline, having plotted it with his buddy. It had been a successful venture all around.

The next day he headed out again, with a different buddy, and they used the track laid the previous day to get out to the best fishing spot on the lake. Our two younger daughters wanted to walk out on the ice to Daddy, as they have done in seasons past. I called him on the cell to verify how much longer he would be out and confirm that they were welcome. He said of course, but gave one word of caution: make sure they stay in my path! He knew if they followed his directions, they would arrive safely. They bundled up and I watched them from our yard. He stood up from his fishing spot and watched over their journey until they arrived safely at his side.

...just like our walk with Father God! We possess the freedom of choice to follow a successful path laid out by the One Who knows where the pitfalls are~ or not. We choose our own degree of success in this life by how closely we follow the path and guidelines Jesus laid out for us. The Bible, the internal witness of the Holy Spirit and spiritual mentors shine the light for our path. Father God stands, watching over our journey until we arrive safely at His side.

Father God, thank You for a fresh, new day, and all the promise it holds! Father, I choose today to do what I know to do, to listen for Your voice, and to follow in Your footsteps. I don't want to "go through the ice!" I ask for vision to see Your steps and wisdom to place my feet securely.

In Jesus' Name, Amen

Transforming Power!

And do not be conformed to this world, but be transformed by the renewing of your mind, that you may prove what is the good and acceptable and perfect will of God. (Romans 12:2)

There have been many times in my career in sales that I have had my mentors and trainers tell me things like "Keep your mind on the things you want, and off of things you don't want!" or "Read a good book to work on developing you!" Isn't it awesome though, to read in God's self help book, the Bible, that He wants us to do the same?

God wants us to not be focused on the things of this world but becoming more like Him by focusing on Him and His Word. I have read many books in my life (hundreds) but I have never found a book that gives me the same comfort, confidence, stability or promises that the Bible does. Every day, I read about promises that were made to me, gifts that were left, or given to me and that eternity is mine with Him!

I don't know about you, but that will transform your thinking every day! Regardless of how bad the day is or what happens, that attitude and belief system will bring you through the pain. I am not saying that pain won't happen, it will: we live in a fallen world. But with the knowledge that comes from not conforming to this world, but transforming your thinking to God's Word, we make it through and do it with a positive attitude!

God's will for our lives is perfect. He has the plan for you and me, and we need to spend more time on that plan and less time on our own!

Challenge: Get a copy of either The One Year Bible or another guide to take you through the whole thing, and begin the journey today to read your way through the entire Bible. My journey has been a tremendous, eye opening experience about what God's will for my life is.

> *Almighty God, thank You for today and the magnificent world that You have created for us to experience. We choose to get closer to You by reading Your Word and listening for Your still small voice. We love You Father! Help us get closer to You!!*
>
> *In Jesus' Name, Amen*

Emotions

Lord, if You had been here, my brother would not have died..." When Jesus saw her weeping, He was deeply moved in spirit and troubled... Jesus wept... Jesus, once more deeply moved, came to the tomb. (John 11:32b, 33, 35, 38)

How often have you been in a painful spot in life, and wondered if your cries ever made it to Heaven, or if the ceiling of your room absorbed them? This Bible section, detailing the death of Lazarus, shows His compassion and humanity. The shortest verse in the Bible is also one of the most powerful~ John 11:35: "Jesus wept." In looking back at the rest of the story, He knew before He made it to Bethany that Lazarus was dead. He also knew that He would use the power of God to raise him back to life. Knowing this, why cry about it? Why not just raise him up and get it over with? I believe it's because, as Hebrews 4:15 makes so plain: "For we do not have a High Priest (Jesus, our mediator) Who is unable to sympathize with our weaknesses, but we have One who has been tempted in every way, just as we are- yet without sin."

Jesus knew the full range of human emotion. He experienced them all. He cried when He lost a friend He dearly loved. He cried when He saw friends He cared for deep in the pain of what they viewed as permanent loss. It troubled His own spirit to see the agony they experienced, and He shared in that pain right along with them. You see, Jesus isn't calloused to our emotions. They are given to us by God and validated by the fact that Jesus had them too; they completed His experience as a man here on earth.

It's important in our view of Who Jesus is, to know that when we are at our weakest point, crying out in either physical or emotional pain, that we don't have a God who stands up and says "Oh brush it off, suck it up, and move on, you cry-baby!" but instead we serve a God Who says "Bring me your cares, hurts and pains. I care for you and will tend this wound for you. Let's move forward together in the fullness of God's power", picks us up, brushes us off, and sets us firmly in place with Him and His power, giving us the ability to stand through any storm or trial this old world can hurl our direction.

Father God, thank You for understanding my emotions on the deepest level. Thank You for picking me up, cleaning my wounds, and restoring me once again. I love You! May I experience the full range of God-given emotions with You by my side, and experience the fullness of Your power to stand and honor You through all the storms of this world!

In Jesus' Name, Amen

Categories

And without faith it is impossible to please God, because anyone who comes to Him must believe that He exists and that He rewards those who earnestly seek Him. (Hebrews 11:6)

I was struck by this passage today as I read it. It takes three parts to receive rewards from God. First of all, we must believe He exists. If He's not there to begin with, it makes sense that there is no reward.

Secondly, we must believe He rewards His people. There are thousands of people who will easily say "of course I believe in God", yet they walk round with no reward, in pain, poverty, & lack of peace because they don't ask for, expect or look for any reward. They believe their only reward will be "someday when they reach those pearly gates". As a result, they let the enemy steal from them and don't even put up the whimper of a fight, because they don't expect any rewards here on earth. Some take it to the extreme, that God doesn't want to give rewards in this life, denying the reality of most of the New Testament, which spells out the blessings of the New Covenant.

Thirdly, He rewards those who earnestly seek Him. To know that there is some reward in life is helpful, and puts us on the right track pointed in the right direction, but stops short of the abundance of reward He has planned for those who follow hard after Him.

It's easy for Christians to agree that salvation is reward for being a Christ-follower, but in reality, that's just the beginning! He put in Covenant Writing for us ~the Bible~ that the New Covenant encompasses the Old, or Original Covenant too. When we choose one, He gives us both! What a bonus! We are in line for "all the promises of Abraham" as well as heaven, as well as having the power of the Holy Spirit in our lives, as well as "having the mind of Christ", as we pursue the One Who loves us with an unending, unconditional love and desires to bless us until we feel overwhelmed, blown away, flooded with His presence!

Which category are you in today?

Father God, I desire to be in the third category, knowing You, looking for, and expecting Your blessings. I want to experience both the New Covenant and Old Covenant blessings. Show me how to follow hard after You so I can experience it all!

In Jesus' Name, Amen

Love Allows the Tough Choice

"This day I call heaven and earth as witnesses against you that I have set before you life and death, blessings and curses. Now choose life so that you and your children may live and that you may love the Lord your God, listen to His voice and hold fast to Him. For the Lord is your life and He will give you many years in the land He swore to give to your fathers, Abraham, Isaac and Jacob." (Deuteronomy 20:19-20)

God so very much wants to give us the very best! He is madly, crazy in love with you, today, right now! He's not some distant Guy who set the world in motion and then kicked back in a chaise lounge with an umbrella drink, peering over His sunglasses every now and then to see what's up in your life periodically. Nor is He a Sovereign who requires no interaction with you in order for you to receive: He doesn't just back up a dump truck at your front door, drop off the blessings in a big pile and leave you to sort through them all as He waves and pulls out of your driveway. No! He wants to partner with you so you're ready and able to accept all He has to give and fully put them to use to get the most out of them!

In other words you and I get to daily choose what level of interaction we will allow Him to have in our lives. Moses was very clear in his statement to the Israelites: life or death, blessing or curses. Go ahead~ pick one!

Just because this is an Old Testament (pre-Jesus) passage doesn't mean it is nullified; actually it means the daily choices we make are more potent than ever! Jesus didn't come to eliminate the Old Covenant, but to fulfill it, simplify it and strengthen it, giving its promises more impact than ever. What, in the Old Covenant, was just for Abraham's biological family lineage, is now open to all of us who accept Jesus~ through faith in Him we are in line for all those blessings of that first covenant... and more!

Once we make that choice to ask Jesus to live in us and be our Lord, the presence of the Holy Spirit inside each of us is a down payment, a deposit, of the eternal life promised us. God has given us a power beyond ourselves to make those daily right choices... without exception! Our choice is this: will we avail ourselves of the Holy Spirit power residing inside us from the Throne Room of Heaven in order to do so?

A man named Paul, who brought this message of hope and Good News to the non-Jews for the very first time, put it this way in the New Testament: "My grace is sufficient for you, for My power is made perfect in weakness." 2 Corinthians 12:9a

> *Father God, I want so very much daily to choose life, daily to choose blessing! I know my weaknesses better than anyone else besides You. I'm thankful that in my weakness Your strength is made perfect, because there's no doubt I can't do this on my own! Be strong in me, oh God. I choose to activate the power of the Holy Spirit living in me in order to make daily life choices that honor You.*

> *In Jesus' Name, Amen*

God Did It!!

*Men of Israel, listen to this: Jesus of Nazareth was a man accred-
ited by God to you by miracles, wonders and signs which God did
among you through Him as you yourselves know. (Acts 2:22)*

*I tell you the truth, anyone who has faith in Me will do
what I have been doing. He will do even greater things than
these because I am going to the Father. (John 14:12)*

How often have you read in Acts about the cool stuff the young
Church (not building, but Body of Christ) did? Or have you looked at the
life of Jesus, and said "wow, He said we could do the same stuff but I don't
see that doing those miracles is a possibility in my life! Jesus was God, the
Disciples knew Him personally and received the tongues of fire~ I didn't,
so how could I do those things?" Perhaps you've even been taught that
from the pulpit, as part of a denomination's religious belief that miracles,
signs and wonders were for "back then~ not now."

The challenge with us as people is that we tend to "shrink to fit" when
it comes to our dreams or our philosophy and our theology: we don't see
it happening around us and can't explain it, so it must not be real even
though we read it in the Bible. We tend to self-impose boundaries for our

own comfort, staying safe in what we know through personal experience. Or perhaps other people imposed their limitations and expectations on us at an early age; even if we didn't agree then, we made them our own over time~ internalized them~ in the belief we had no real choice on the matter. God says we do have choice, and He will renew our minds to get rid of the old tapes, shed the old limitations. He will give us new eyes to see, new ears to hear, and a new heart to understand what the Bible actually says!

Today's verse says God did the miraculous stuff Jesus is credited with. Jesus' part of the equation was to spend time with the Father and be properly aligned with Him. From that posture, Jesus was able to understand the plan and make Himself available to do the things God said needed to be done.

Think about that for a moment: If the only reason Jesus was able to do all of His cool stuff (miracles, deliverance, healings) here in earth was because He was God, then you and I have no chance to live up to His own words! Why would He set us up for failure by telling us we would do not only the same stuff... but greater things?? It would be completely unfair and downright mean to set us up for such drastic failure! If, however, Jesus operated in complete harmony with Father God and Holy Spirit, then that's a different story! If Jesus modeled complete surrender in the expectation that we would follow His example because God's same power was available to us also, then we also are capable of living like He did!

God doesn't promise without being able to deliver on it~ ever. If He did, and violated His perfection even once, His perfection would cease to be. We wouldn't be able to trust Him about anything He said! Either we can take Him at His Word, or we cannot. Either we allow Him to illuminate the Word to our hearts and stretch to grow into the fullness of what He has for us, or we "shrink to fit" and in so doing deny His created, stated destiny for us. That's our choice.

Father God, may I not "shrink to fit"! Light up Your Word in my
life so my heart is receptive and I am postured properly before You.
Only then can we work together to flip this world upside down!

In Jesus' Name, Amen

A Child Again...

(Jesus said) "Let the little children come to Me, and do not hinder them"... and He took the children in His arms put His hands on them and blessed them. (Mark 10:14-15)

I tell you the truth, unless you change and become like little children, you will never enter the kingdom of heaven. (Matthew 18:3)

This morning I woke up to the squeals of laughter and pitter-pattering of eight sets of little feet, as opposed to the typical three sets of my own little girls. The warming scent of coffee wafts through the air, sunshine sparkles off the fresh powder-snow and streams into our home. It's an unusual morning, since we had two families over for the weekend and they got snowed in for an extra night when the highway closed! Even though everyone had been here since Friday, Monday holds a new glee especially for the kids since it was an unexpected gift!

Their joy of the simple things reminds us as adults of the basics of life. Jesus loves children! In fact, He taught that to enter the Kingdom of Heaven, we need to be like them. There's an innocent trust that they carry, especially in early childhood. They don't worry about bills, the economy or unemployment. They trust that their needs will be provided for by

Mom and Dad: food will be on the table, clothes will be clean and keep them warm, we will pick them up, hold them, always love them, and our kisses hold a special power to make the damage of the skinned knees all better~ they have simple faith.

That's the way God wants us to rely on Him. He's the best Daddy in the universe! God created us to live in families as a visible human illustration of the relationship His heart desires with us. Just as we want so very much to give good things to our kids despite our faults, so He desires to give good gifts to us~ and more because of His perfect holiness. So often we complicate it. How many times have you caught yourself saying "I want to pray, but after what I did last night I don't deserve to", or "I want to trust God with that promotion opportunity, but does He really care about it with all the serious tragedies in the world?"

Hey~ you need to know He does care, He does want the best for you, and when you have asked for and received forgiveness for whatever yesterday held, your pathway to Him is clear. Simply trust His goodness. Take time today to be a child with your Heavenly Daddy. Talk to Him about what's on your heart. Get to a quiet place in your heart and just pour it all out to Him. Share your hopes, give Him your cares, listen to Him, and tell Him you choose to trust Him moment by moment as you walk through your day together.

Dear Father, Thank You for simple trust and joy! Thank you that You enjoy my "joyful noise"! Thank you for the opportunity to curl up on Your lap and pour out my heart to You today, whatever my circumstance. Today I chose to trust You with it all, moment by moment.

In Jesus' Name, Amen

More than a Hallmark

For God so loved the world that He gave His only Son! (John 3:16)

I pray that you, being rooted and established in love, may have power...
to grasp how wide and long and high and deep is the love of Christ,
and to know this love that surpasses knowledge... (Ephesians 3:17-18)

As we near Valentine's Day, stores fill with displays full gift ideas for "that special someone". It can be a fabulous holiday, or it can strike a shot of loneliness into the passers-by. Emotions evoked range from the warm blush of first love, the pain of first break-up, hopeful anticipation of attention from the one you have your eye on, dismay at the approach of that first Valentine's Day alone since divorce or death of a spouse, all the way to celebration of a deep love well-tended for years.

Regardless of your current Hallmark status as Valentine's Day approaches, and whether or not I personally have your address, there's one Valentine I can guarantee you of, and that's from your Heavenly Father, Who happens to be absolutely crazy about you!!! He won't bring you chocolates or flowers, but He will bring you companionship, peace, wise counsel, joy, love, strength, comfort, a listening ear, healing, and freedom. All this is for you to enjoy here, on top of the custom-built mansion He has for you later, while you're lavished in all the riches abounding in heaven!

You mean so much to Him that His love letter, the Bible, is sixty-six books, not pages, long! He wants you to know Him completely~ no holds barred, no games. He will never lie to you, cheat on you, or leave you alone. He is thoroughly trustworthy, and His ultimate desire is for you to be complete, not lacking anything! God's love surpasses every thing this world has to offer. As amazing the love I have for my girls it pales in comparison to the ultimate love God provides at the deepest level of my being. Because He is God, He can provide that for you, too, without ever running out of any of those gifts mentioned earlier!

Chocolates end up on your hips, stuffed animals become worn, and flowers fade, but your worth to Him is immeasurable, unfathomable, limitless, undisputed, completely unconditional, never-ending. You are unique, a one-of-a-kind masterpiece, priceless, unduplicatable, unprecedented in His heart! You are loved!

Father God, I thank you for Your love for me! Take me to the next level in my relationship with You so I can love You back better and experience more of what You have for me. I trust You with all my heart!

In Jesus' Name, Amen.

Better Results from Prayer!

*Now the serpent was more crafty than any of the wild animals the
Lord God had made. He said to the woman, "Did God really say,
'You must not eat from any tree in the garden'?" (Genesis 3:1)*

*"Do not be afraid, Daniel. Since the first day that you set your
mind to gain understanding and to humble yourself before God
your words were heard, and I have come in response to them. But
the prince of the Persian kingdom resisted me twenty-one days.
Then Michael, one of the chief princes, came to help me, because
I was detained there... Now I have come..." (Daniel 10:12-14)*

*(Jesus said) "Let us go over to the other side."...A furi-
ous squall came up... He got up, rebuked the wind and
said to the waves, "Quiet! Be still!" (Mark 4:35-39)*

*"Therefore I tell you, whatever you ask for in prayer, believe
that you have received it, & it will be yours. (Mark 11:24)*

We do not want you to become lazy, but to imitate those who through faith and patience inherit what has been promised. (Hebrews 6:12)

For we walk by faith and not by sight. (2 Corinthians 5:7)

Oh, that's a whole bunch of verses! I figure the devo itself can be a bit shorter that way, allowing you to dig in as much as you care to on your own, but I believe these are necessary to complete today's concepts.

Have you ever wondered if there was something you could do to get more of your prayers answered? Well, actually there are a number of things, and this is not an exhaustive discussion of that, by any means, but will highlight some issues. Since we have faith in Jesus, it only makes sense that we want see results from the time we spend praying, right?

Mark 11 gives several pointers on praying prayers that change circumstances producing results. The one I want you to note today is this: we must believe when we ask~ not when we see the result. "Unbelief is a cancer to our answered prayers!", in the wise words of Pastor Jerry Dirmann. All the prayers we pray in accordance with God's will He wants to answer, but sometimes our mouth can be our own worst enemy, and of course the real enemy is happy to help us with that. Take a look at Genesis: Satan's first tactic was to get Eve off of God's Word and cause her to question Him. Once she took that fall, the rest was easy: she quit standing on what God said, and started looking at current circumstances, listening to another voice. Without the Absolute in place, the rest was just shifting sand.

Have you heard him whispering in your ear, trying to get you into doubt about a promise you're holding on to? Go back to the promise God highlighted to you and the Scripture that you are standing on. Bring it to Him, come "back to center" and renew yourself in His Word.

Do you think the opposition you're facing, whether it's other people, or circumstances, is an evidence of a "closed door" from God, even though at one point you were so sure of what you heard from Him? Take a look at the first reference in Mark: Jesus had said "let's cross over", showing His full intent to arrive, but the storm came~ so bad that the men who made their living on the sea thought that they were going to die! Did that mean that God had changed His mind and Jesus was to turn around and go back?? No! It meant there was opposition: He needed to step up, use His authority and shut it down. (By the way, if you've been reading along with us, you know that He used the same authority that's been given to us as well).

One reason we need to continue in our faith is that while God's desire is to meet every right request we make, many times we quit praying or standing on the promise before we see the results... even though the answer is on its way! Check out the passage in Daniel. The angel was dispatched the very first day Daniel began to pray, with the answer he was looking for. The enemy was directly the cause of delay. Daniel stood twenty-one days waiting... but knew the answer was coming! Sometimes we must wait for the answer. Waiting isn't any fun, especially in the instant, microwave-world we live in now. One huge difference I want to point out for you is this: human patience can be translated as to "we'll just wait and see". But Biblical patience translates to standing in expectation on His Word :"I believe it! I believe it! Regardless of the circumstances I know my God will come through!" See the Hebrews verse? Faith and patience: active waiting, not just "Oh whatever God wants to do or when He cares to show up in my life." Where is the faith in that?? or the expectation? or the promise being stood upon? There isn't any! God says His promises will come to pass, that we have received what we've asked for in faith when we believe it and build ourselves up in our faith during the waiting process. Dr. Chuck Pierce says it this way: "faith is the pause between knowing what God's plan is and seeing it actually take place". If we let go of our faith in the middle of that pause, how can we expect to receive the answer?

Hmmm... I know I don't want to be caught in that gap! I don't want you to be, either. How about we work together to strengthen and encourage each other to stay strong, holding fast to what God has promised, regardless of what wave-crashing, boat-swamping circumstances we face? I'm liking the sound of that!!

> *Father God, in the midst of rough waters, I choose to hold on to You and Your promises! I choose to encourage myself in Your Word, building up my faith and to help do the same for others. I will wait with "Biblical patience", using the authority You gave and staying with what I know You have said in Your Word.*
>
> *In Jesus' Name, Amen*

The Box and The Cross

...but in your hearts set apart Christ as Lord. Always be prepared to give an answer to everyone who asks you to give the reason for the hope that you have. But do this with gentleness and respect. (Peter 3:15)

I have a dear friend named John. He is a gentle man with strong hands, a big heart and a huge love for his GOD.

The other day he was on a two-block walk when he encountered a man carrying, or should I say struggling to carry, a big heavy box. As the men drew nearer to each other, John's intent was to help him carry it. Before he reached John, however the man reached his limit and set the box quickly down onto the sidewalk.

John hurriedly approached him to offer help, and as he did his cross necklace caught the other man's eye. He looked up at John and said "Is that cross you're wearing real, or is it just for show?"

John confidently replied "Oh, it's real all right!"

"Then pray for me", said the man.

John did, right there on the spot. The man then picked his box back up and continued on his way.

Such a short interaction, yet such a stunning moment! John was ready with his answer when the question came. Are you? We are commended to be ready with an answer, in season and out, at a moment's notice.

This other man could have been an angel. Or this man could have simply been another human being struggling with the weight of his load, in need of encouragement before he could go on. People like that are everywhere around us. John knew the Source of that strength and encouragement! May we follow his example and be so ready.

Lord, give me eyes to see those around me struggling with a heavy load. Give me a heart willing to help and ready to cry out to You on behalf of another at a moment's notice, even- no, especially- in the middle of the sidewalks of life.

In Jesus' Name, Amen

There's A Revolution Coming!

Behold I am coming soon! My reward is with Me and I will give to everyone according to what he has done. (Revelation 22:12)

There's a revolution coming! Can you feel it??

The Bible tells us that in the end days there will be a major outpouring of the Holy Spirit. The speed of Bible prophecy being fulfilled will increase. People who don't know Jesus will lack peace and experience turmoil as they look at world events, the crumbling economic base, natural disasters and falling-apart families.

As a Believer, you are in position for these days to help bring hope to those who don't yet know the Author of your peace, the Perfector of your faith. Lives hang in the balance~ sometimes their very eternity is in your hands; will you step out of Comfortable and risk bringing Life to someone else?

Does that make you feel a bit queasy? Good! On your own this is too big a task. The good news is: God doesn't expect or ask you to do it on your own, but by the power of His might, by the Holy Spirit living inside of you!

Here's a real-life, modern-day example: a friend of mine sat in his office one day and this certain guy's name kept coming to mind. He knew he needed to call him: it was already on his "to do" list in a later timeslot on his agenda. The next time the name came, he recognized a sense of urgency, that there was a reason God was laying this name on his heart right then. He picked up the phone immediately...

...on the other end of the line came a very startled voice: the guy in question had fallen asleep at the wheel while driving, and woke up to this call... in the lane across the median for oncoming traffic, about fifty feet from a tree on the embankment! The reason for the sense of urgency was immediately apparent.

Had he pushed it off any longer it would have been too late. Had he responded to the first prompting, perhaps the guy would not have fallen asleep at all and the situation not have held any drama to it at all as he rode safely down the proper lane of traffic.

We don't always get that in-your-face understanding of why God puts someone on our hearts, but it doesn't mean it's not important to obey. We don't always have that level of understanding as to why those words were in our hearts during a conversation, but our mental understanding isn't the goal... what really matters, when all is said and done, is that we DID what we were told to do. We chose to live at peace as much as it depended on us. We chose to forgive when put in the situation of offense. We chose to stand up for our values against the crowd in a respectful manner. We chose to love when it wasn't easy at all... and because of our obedient choices, someone's life is changed and our minds and hearts are clean before God. Someone saw Christ in us in the middle of our handling of a crisis- either ours or theirs. They saw our peace and heard the Father through our voices. Their eyes were opened, their lives changed.

The line of hope we offer to others is sometimes quietly lived, undiscovered until years later; at other times it's as stark as the above example. Either way we need to realize: time is short and lives hang in the balance.

There are times eternity literally is in your hands. Will you allow the God of the universe to use you, and step into your destiny?

> *Father God, to partner with You sounds uncanny and I struggle with the idea of being worthy to partner with You. I'm thankful You see me as holy like Jesus since I accepted Your gifts of forgiveness and restoration. Please strengthen me with a proper boldness to step into my destiny and turn someone's life toward You today!*
>
> *In Jesus' Name, Amen*

God Bless You!

All these blessings will come upon you if you obey the
Lord your God... (Deuteronomy 28:2-14)

Someone next to you sneezes and everyone around says... you guessed it, "Bless you!" Some brave soul may venture "God bless you!" Have you ever wondered what that means? Superstition used to hold that someone's soul could leave them during a sneeze, hence the request for God to bless them so they neither dropped over dead, nor become inhabited by something other than their own original spirit.

Have you ever asked "what is 'blessing' supposed to be anyway?" Nothing short of "the tangible touch of God"! How cool is that?

How would your life change if you lived each day looking for God's tangible touch, since you have asked Him into your heart and are in right standing with Him, having accepted Jesus' righteousness as your own? What would that do to your awareness of your surroundings? How would you be able to impact others as you share this profound knowledge, knowing God is not only able but willing to touch your life in a daily, personal way? I think it's safe to say your hope, sense of expectation and peace would be contagious!

How would your life change others if you walked through it declaring to other people the tangible, powerful, life-changing touch of God? From your posture of being filled with God's blessings you can then extend them to others by saying "God bless your day!" instead of just saying "have a good one!"

In John 10:10 we see that the enemy is the one out to destroy us and steal from us, but God sent Jesus in order to give us life so abundant that we can't contain it all and the natural outcome is to pass it on, give it away, multiplying it from a thankful heart!

Whether it's a cup of coffee or a tall iced tea, we can each picture our drink of choice reaching the rim and tumbling over into a waterfall of liquid, spreading quickly across the table as the "extra" splashes beyond the borders of the glass or coffee cup, can't we? The cup is still full, but the drink has had an impact beyond its original capacity.

That's how God wants it to be with us! He wants to touch our lives in such powerful, stirring, intimate ways that the blessings which accompany His touch overflow into the lives of those we touch, even in a quick pass-by on the street! We are His goblet, or glass, or coffee cup, and through us His plan is to touch the world~ and that's nothing to sneeze at! Be blessed, and go bless~ give the tangible touch of God!

Dear God, thank you for Your desire to touch my life! The thought of impacting others for You can be intimidating, but my heart is to overflow for You. Show me how to see Your tangible touch in my own life and then be able to give it away so You get the glory!

In Jesus' Name, Amen

Steeped Like Tea

My purpose is that they (Christians) may be encouraged in heart and united in love, so that they may have the FULL riches of complete understanding, in order that they may know the mystery of God, namely Christ, in whom are hidden ALL the treasures of wisdom and knowledge. I tell you this so that no one may deceive you by fine-sounding arguments. (Colossians 2:2-4)

How does all that sound? Does your heart need some encouragement today? How about unity- wouldn't it be a great change of pace to not have fighting or strife at family gatherings or the company party? How would it feel to have all the treasures of wisdom and knowledge to overcome life's challenges? In this day and age of shrouded truth and thinly veiled lies, wouldn't it be great to never be deceived again?

Those things are the ultimate goal, yet left to ourselves, it's just a pie-in-the-sky concept, completely unattainable. With Christ and His Word dwelling (residing) in us richly, the tables turn. What used to be out of reach comes within our grasp! "How?" you may ask.

We do our part, spending time with our Loving Creator, Who has given us all authority and power necessary to reign as kings this side of heaven. We pray/ speak out our hearts and worship to Him. We read His

Instruction Manual and think on it throughout the day. We trust Him and hear His voice for a fresh "download" for the new day ahead.

Will we completely accomplish this goal perfectly on the earth- side of heaven? No, but we can make serious progress towards it, and the peace of Christ will rule and reign in our hearts as we choose it to, as we step forward one moment at a time, toward the completion of our destiny. Dare to go for it! Let your emotions be renewed, your heart healed from the junk of the world, and your mind be transformed, by thinking about the verse He highlights to you today. Mull it over in your mind, let it ~ let Him~ sink in to the deeper places of your being, like tea steeping in its cup, the aroma of your transforming life fragrantly soothing to those you love... and even those you don't in your natural state.

Know Christ. Full of wisdom and knowledge. Encourager of others and promoter of unity. Complete in your understanding. Wow, imagine your life like that! Do you want it? It's there for you! Don't be deceived by religious leaders that say you can't know Christ, that His will is an unexplainable mystery that can't be known; keep it in context! Rather have your mind renewed and your heart transformed by Him ~ according to His Word it is possible!

Father God, I choose to be renewed by You! I dare to
trust you one moment at a time. Steep in me like tea. I
want the fullness of You and Your understanding.

In Jesus' Name, Amen

Covenant Assurance

He who dwells in the shelter of the Most High WILL rest in the
shadow of the Almighty. I will say of the Lord, "He IS my refuge and
my fortress, my God, in Whom I trust." Surely He WILL save you
from the fowler's snare and from the deadly pestilence. He WILL
cover you with His feathers, and under His wings you WILL find
refuge; His faithfulness WILL be your shield and rampart...

...IF you make the Most High your dwelling- even the
Lord Who is my refuge- THEN no harm will befall
you, no disaster will come near your tent...

..."Because he loves Me," says the Lord, "I WILL rescue him, for
he acknowledges My Name. He WILL call on Me and I WILL
answer him; I WILL deliver him and honor him." (Psalm 91)

Please go read the whole chapter, but look at how much assurance
is given in just these select passages of this one chapter! Is it any wonder
why this is a favorite of so many people, a most-quoted chapter during
crisis and times needing protection? God leaves no room for doubt as

to His actions on behalf of those who love Him and acknowledge His Name, respecting His Word.

Do you know Him in this sense? Have you experienced His closest presence and protection, or the peace in the midst of crisis? If not, you need to know that it is possible. It is His heart's desire for you: to be in such tight relationship with Him that you have the same confidence in His Word that the author who penned these words did.

You see, waaayyy back in the beginning of the Bible, in the Old Testament, God entered into blood covenant with a man named Abraham and his family~ a group of people that He made the strongest of commitments to. That commitment was more than a contract; it became a way of life. Blood Covenant is the most binding situation you can find yourself in. It means you and your covenant partner defend each other until any enemy is defeated... or you die yourself.

Because God is spirit, He had no blood to shed to confirm the covenant like Abraham did, so He orchestrated history and sent Jesus~ God in the form of man~ who could confirm the covenant with blood. He was so totally determined to show us the great lengths to which He would go to partner with us that Jesus didn't just contribute one or two drops of blood; but He gave it all, allowing Himself to be sacrificed on our behalf. Now He has done His part. Psalm 91 shows us what His intent is toward those of us who have entered into covenant with Him. It's pretty solid, isn't it?

Do you wish to access it? You can! Verses 1 and 9 tell us to make Him and His shelter our "dwelling place", not a term we use today, but it means our hang-out place. It's where we go, where we live. He is Who we turn to when all the chips are stacked against us and we feel alone. He is Who we celebrate with during the good times. There's an ebb and flow of give and take in the relationship. We know He's got our back- no matter what- when we connect with Him like this. He's not just a "get out of hell free" card! He is madly, crazy in love with you and ready to prove it!

Father God, my Blood Covenant Partner, my Shield, my Shel-
ter, my Refuge, my Peace, my Fortress, unstoppable, absolute, sure,
impenetrable, my Savior! I want to know You in the ebb and flow
of relationship where I know You are sure to back me because
I'm in right relationship with You, and we are inseparable!

In Jesus' Name, Amen

His Love is Seen in the Details

"Make a table of acaia wood- two cubits long, a cubit wide and a cubit and a half high. Overlay it with pure gold and make a gold molding... (Exodus 25:23)

"Leave here, turn eastward and hide in the Kerith Ravine, east of the Jordan. You will drink from the brook, and I have ordered the ravens to feed you there." (I Kings 17:3-4)

"For I know the plans I have for you," declares the Lord, plans to prosper you and not to harm you, plans to give you a hope and a future..." (Jeremiah 29:11)

You may be wondering "What do these verses have to do with each other? How do they tie in to make any sense? I see three different time periods, three different authors, three different characters. What are you doing?" They are more different than alike, for sure. But that just goes to reinforce the point I want to make with them: God lays out specific plans for each of us. He doesn't want our lives left to chance or lived haphazardly!

He was so incredibly detailed to Moses with the plans for the Tabernacle that it can be almost tenuous to read... yet if He is that detailed with a building, how much more detailed is He with you, the one who is not an inanimate object, but carefully fashioned in His own likeness??

The passage about Elijah shows again in great detail how and where God had planned to provide food and water for His man in the middle of famine and drought, not leaving him to fend for himself in the midst of a judgment from God that was on everyone else for their disobedience. He knows our human needs, and makes provision for them, not overlooking them. These are not lost details on the vast landscape of the universe!

Also, to Jeremiah, God gave His reassurance not only that He has plans for His people, but that they are for good, to prosper us, to give us hope, so we can have a future!

This statement was not just a matter of fact for the original person it was spoken to so many years ago, but also one for us to hold on to today. God is the same yesterday today and forever. His promises to us who call on His Name are "yes" and "amen"! The promises of God are timeless, and unending. They are for each of us: they are for you, today, right now, right here, at this moment and the next one too... Ponder that. Let that sink into your psyche... meditate there for a while. Let it renew you, restore you, refresh you. You are not forgotten nor overlooked, nor unprepared for.

Father God, thank You for planning ahead and making provision for me. Thank You that I am not forgotten. Thank You for the details You designed for my life.

In Jesus' Name, Amen

No More Condemnation!

*There is therefore now NO CONDEMNATION to
those which are in Christ Jesus! (Romans 8:1)*

How does that sound for a change? Pretty good? In the mainstream news, and in many jobs, the unfortunate truth is that condemnation is rampant. How awesome of our God to say that's not how ~ or Who~ He is! That's just not how He does business; it's not His character! In case we missed it the first time, He tells us again in John 3:17 "For God did not send His Son (Jesus) into the world to condemn the world, but that the world, through Him, might be saved!"

Is this too much for you? So many religious structures of our day pile heaps of guilt and condemnation onto sincere believers seeking freedom and forgiveness from sin, and leave their church experience feeling worse than before, which is tragic! The enemy knows shame and guilt are easily manipulated emotions, and he exploits them to the best of his evil ability. The last thing he wants is your freedom, your peace, and the Truth of God's love shining into your heart. One of his favorite tactics, if he's already lost you to believing in Christ's forgiveness of past sins, is to keep you captive to condemnation that ties you to sins you commit after you have received Christ (Oh, I should have known better! Why did I do that again??) a feeling of unworthiness~ unworthiness to receiving the rest, the fullness, of what God, through the high sacrifice of Jesus, died to restore to you!

There is a proper place for the Holy Spirit to nudge you when you head in the wrong direction. Many people call it your conscience. It's God's warning system to keep you in the center of His will, however the difference between Him and the enemy is this: when you stray off the path and ask for it, God gives forgiveness right away! You don't have to wonder if He was true to His Word. You don't have to feel guilty any longer than it takes for the words of confession and "please forgive me" to leave your lips. It's done! Gone ~into His "sea of forgetfulness" as the Bible calls it. Beat the enemy of your soul with the Truth of God's Word, which He gave you for just such occasions as enemy harassment. God's Word is a powerful two-edged sword, able to tear down any strongholds in your life! Use it as such! Cut off the condemning voice of the enemy!

Dear Father, thank you for Your heart that loves me and is for me, regardless of the mistakes I've made. Thank you for the power of for-giveness that overcomes all my sin through the blood of Jesus and wipes away all condemnation that would separate me from You! Lord, I pray that You will restore me and give me a vision of how You see me in Christ~ worthy, holy, pure and able to be used for Your pur-poses and glory! Thank You, In Jesus' most precious Name, Amen!

Sin Condemned Not People!

And so he condemned sin in sinful man... (Romans 8:3b)

So many times people mistakenly think God is mad at them. They picture Him as a mean old ogre in the sky, full of anger and judgement. They know right from wrong, they know they made bad choices, and feel guilty and unworthy to come ask for forgiveness thinking they'll get zapped by some heavenly lightening bolt on their approach. Nothing could be further from the truth! God doesn't condemn people, He condemns sin!

How the enemy loves it when we get it wrong! The whole reason God sent Jesus to die on the cross is because of His love for people, and His unwillingness that we should go to hell, separated from Him forever. His condemnation He reserves for sin~ not the ones He created, and whose futures He planned, and whose hairs He even has numbered! The "Good News" is that Jesus paid the price for sin: He became sin for us, even though He himself never sinned!

Sin is willful disobedience to God. One sin is all that it takes to keep us from heaven. Being better than your neighbor doesn't help you make the cut~ God doesn't grade on a curve. Knowing that, when we're honest with ourselves, we know that our attitudes and actions haven't always been pure, don't we? The message of the Good News is that it only took one drop of Jesus' blood to pay the price for you (and me), but He loved you sooo much that He allowed His body to be emptied of His blood, so there would be no question about His love for you! Receive His gift: the paid price for your redemption! Shed the thoughts of condemnation. Secure your salvation by accepting what He did; don't let it go to waste and find yourself paying the price for your sin~ that's not at all what He intended!

Father God, Thank You for the gift of Jesus! I receive it, I receive Him! Thank You for the blood that paid the price for my sin, and bridged the gap between me and You! Thank You that the gift of Jesus' blood eliminated my sin from the equation, and now I can stand before You forgiven, and place in me the burning desire to share the Good News with those who need to know You. In Jesus' Name, Amen

Flex Your Muscles!

Is any one of you in trouble? He should pray. Is anyone happy? Let him sing songs of praise. Is anyone of you sick? He should call the elders of the church to pray over him and anoint him with oil in the name of the Lord. And the prayer offered in faith will make the sick person well; the Lord will raise him up. If he has sinned, he will be forgiven. Therefore confess your sins to each other and pray for each other so that you may be healed. The prayer of a righteous man is powerful and effective. (James 5:13-16)

"Have faith in God", Jesus answered. "I tell you the truth, if anyone says to this mountain, 'Go, throw yourself into the sea', and does not doubt in his heart but believes that what he says will happen, it will be done for him. Therefore I tell you, whatever you ask for in prayer, believe that you have received it, and it will be yours. And when you stand praying, if you hold anything against anyone, forgive him, so that your Father in heaven may forgive you your sins." (Mark 11:22-26)

I know there are a lot of italicized words in today's passage; well, that's because there's a lot to it! Just one disclaimer: I can't exhaustively give you everything in these passages in a devo~ to get more, ask for the

Holy Spirit to give you the personal revelation! I want to head you in the direction of digging in on this one!

Jesus expects that those of us walking in faith and right relationship with God will be visibly separate from the world, and unusually good health is part of that visible difference. Do you remember the documentation of the plagues in Egypt? God differentiated between His people the Israelites, and the Egyptians. It was dark in Egypt, but light in the land of Goshen where the Israelites were quartered. God drew that line again and again throughout their history. Even when the people made it out of Egypt and into the wilderness, not only did their clothes not wear out, but there was not a sick one among them! That's more than just a little amazing for three million people, don't you think??

While God does know how to take care of His own, we also live in a sinful fallen world, and the enemy tries to pervert what the Bible actually says. How many of you have been taught "oh, healing was for back then but not now"? Or had a pastor say to you "well I prayed for so-and-so and he died, so I guess God just doesn't heal anymore". Perhaps you've said, "Okay God, I trust You to heal me of this 'x' " and refused the suggestion of unbelieving relatives who told you to go to the doctor... yet a week later you ended up there anyway... and they smirk. That weakens your faith, so even though your head may be able to quote the verse your heart doesn't have the Faith in it that comes from personal revelation which is what makes it unshakable inside of your spirit.

Today's verses list some things to evaluate when you find yourself wanting to believe, but unsure "how far to take it" in believing God:

- Are you asking in line with His will? (He won't generally honor your request to avoid consequences of wrong behavior that violates principles in His Word)
- Do you believe God, or are you just "sticking your toe in the

water"? (even if you are, there's hope~ so keep reading!)

- Do you ask in confident faith, knowing God has heard you, can do what you ask, and is willing to perform it? (all three parts are important here)
- Have you asked Believing Christian Leaders in authority over you to anoint you, lay hands on you and pray?
- Do you have any unforgiveness in your heart toward anyone, including God? (this is the biggest block to answered prayer, remember The Lord's Prayer?)

Think of it like this: faith is like a muscle, so the more we work out the stronger we get. Same principle here: the more you read and speak out God's Word, the stronger you get, the faster Faith (meaning personal revelation inside you) comes. Don't be discouraged if you don't see an instant answer, soak in His Word, build the muscle.

We can learn a lot from this passage: take a close look at verse 24; the verb-tense changes three times: Believe (present tense), have received (past tense) and will be yours (future tense). What's up with that? Well, we know that Jesus died, rose again and paid for us to not only make it to heaven but also forgave our sins and brought us into the blessings of Abraham. Healing, salvation and forgiveness are part of that~ already complete~ hence the past-tense verb for our current request. The last verb is future-tense: "will be". Some answers from God are instantaneous. Some come as we do the thing He asks us to do to complete our healing, or "as we go" like one passage says. Some healing is more of a process that comes more gradually without fanfare, more quietly and intimately.

So how is your faith muscle? I encourage you to take some time to pray and ponder this topic. How much better to be prepared and already "spiritually fit" for the next enemy campaign against your health before it arrives at your doorstep! You will be able to put it down quickly, rather than finding yourself in a "crash course" to hurry up and get in shape for a fight after the first punch is thrown!

Father God, thank You for the power in Your Word. Reveal to me that You are not only Willing, but Able to heal each: my body, soul and mind, just as You were willing to forgive all my sins. In Your economy, these are already a reality! Lord I want to become "spiritually fit" so I can encourage others and You can be praised in all of the earth!

In Jesus' Name, Amen

A Known God

I sought the Lord and He heard me, He deliv-
ered me from all my fears! (Psalm 34:4)

That sounds pretty good in such days of uncertainty as we are facing now, doesn't it? How many people do you know that have been freed from every fear possible in our generation? I daresay not many. Probably even most Christians we know live with fear of some type.

This verse has been in my head for days. Today, listening to the radio I was reminded of another piece that dovetails nicely with this verse. Corrie Ten Boom, a survivor of one of Germany's worst Holocaust-era concentration camps, said "Never be afraid to trust an unknown future to a known God." I believe the author in Psalms felt the same way as Corrie: they both knew Who they trusted to care for them! God wasn't just a genie-in-the-sky to either of these parties. He was a Friend Who had their best interest at heart~ they were both certain of it! They knew they would be delivered, they learned enough about their God to walk without fear, even when they didn't know the way, or what lay around the next bend in the road of life. They knew God's heart. They had sought Him out, and were secure in their relationship regardless of outer circumstances!

Does this mean they never felt a twinge of fear? I doubt it. But I'm sure that when a situation presented itself, they took it to their God, their Daddy, their Best Friend, and held it up and said "Please help! I know You can!" and He did.

This isn't a lazy confidence. To develop a tough faith that will hold through any storm, requires, you guessed it~ going through the storms... but coming out stronger on the other side.

There's a piece of this verse we can miss in our English language. We say we know something or know someone after reading an article on the internet or seeing a tabloid headline, but the fact of the matter is we don't know that movie star! If we walked up to them and engaged them in conversation they would have no idea who we were! We may know about them, but we don't know who they are on the inside. We may have read an article about reconstructing a car engine, but we don't have the experiential knowledge of actually having done it until... we do it.

Many people today know about God, but how many really know God's heart? How many people truly know that they can trust Him to see them through, regardless of the test results, or the economic this or that? We can know about Him from Sunday's sermon, but what's our understanding of Him on a personal experiential level? Have we studied His Word or talked with Him enough that now we can turn our hurts, fears, ideas, plans, concerns over to Him without a doubt? Have we built on His previous interaction in our lives so now we reduce our hesitation factor to give Him today's concerns more quickly? I hope so!

I know that's where I want to be, in every area of my life. So far it's been quite the journey, but I can tell you I trust Him more today than yesterday, or last year! He's never let me down; He's faithful, and He's delivering me from ALL my fears.

Father, God, Daddy, thank You for Your faithfulness to hear me when I call to You, that I can know You in the midst of all the circumstances life throws my way! I want to know You on an experiential level, not just in the way of head knowledge. I trust You, my known God, with my unknown future, sure that You will deliver me from ALL my fears!

In Jesus' Name, Amen

Part 1 of 2: Suckers and Shooters

All Scripture is God-breathed and is useful for teaching rebuking, correcting and training in righteousness, so that the wo/man of God may be thoroughly equipped for every good work. (2 Timothy 3:16-17)

Train up a child in the way s/he should go, and when s/he is old s/he will not depart from it. (Proverbs 22:6)

When the weather has begun to break here in West Michigan, it means, among other things, time to get into spring clean up! I spent a day out raking the leaves off of our hostas and young pines. The work revealed both suckers coming up near the base of the mature elms, as well as shooters running across the ground, connecting the vines in their criss-cross pattern throughout the yard. It had been a while since I had given the triangle section between the main and service drives much attention, rather I had focused on areas nearer the house, and now it showed!

As I worked with a friend, we talked about our girls, their friends and the choices we saw being made in various areas of life. As we talked, I saw the connection between both types of work: the yard and the parenting. We didn't have to plant the weeds. We didn't plant the suckers, yet here we were clearing them off our property.

I went around our maturing trees, snipping off the suckers that were springing up at their bases. Suckers sap the energy of the primary trees, slowing their growth. If the trees are nearly mature, there's less interference, but for those just getting a good start, suckers can be very damaging.

How like our children is that! We tend to the garden of our children's hearts and lives as our God-given responsibility. We are the protectors of their growth. We monitor who comes in to their lives when they're young and help them determine if the new relationships are healthy, or just "suckers" that sap their strength, distracting their focus. Those that are damaging, we are responsible for snipping~ "you can be casual friends at school, but I'm not comfortable with you spending time at x's house". Others we cultivate and help tend, deeming them healthy and wise. Some fall into the category of, well, we're not sure at the moment, so as parents we reserve the right to keep an eye on the budding relationship, discuss choices and monitor development until we can determine more clearly. We talk through situations in life and how to handle them: "How do you feel when that happens?" "If you said that, would they understand what you meant?" "Is what s/he said or did honoring to God? to her parents?" "What would be a better response next time?" "Is this the sign of a good friend?" "Did you apologize for your part in the problem?" "Do you see the consequences for choosing that behavior?" "What do you think will happen next time?"

My goal is two-fold: first, to come alongside my precious girls helping them identify how they should behave and the healthy attitudes they should have as they grow up. Secondly, to help them evaluate the friendships they're choosing. We all know that those whom we allow to get the closest to us influence us to the greatest degree. We all raise our children with the end goal of being able to release them to their own life equipped for making healthy decisions. It's our parental right and duty to snip the "suckers" we see as unhealthy in our children's lives~ whether it's a person or a habit: children don't come naturally equipped with the perspective to do so. It must be done for them at first, modeled then taught.

We will do well to take them beyond the Golden Rule and introduce them to Jesus, helping them establish that most important relationship, getting them into His Word, modeling prayer at whatever level we are at ourselves, modeling Bible reading, giving them a journal. Realize, parents, as John 10:10 says, that the enemy is come ONLY to steal, kill and destroy. Are you seeing that already in the lives of your kids? Snip it while it's a small problem! You don't have to plant the suckers: they sneak in! Teach your kids to understand Life through the lens of God's Word, so they can live the second part of the verse: Jesus came to bring us abundant life~ and that's for our children, too!

Father God, Thank You for the opportunity to partner with You in this adventure of parenting, that I don't have to "go it alone"! Help me to identify the "suckers" in the lives of my kids so they don't just settle for good, but propel forward toward "best". Thank You that I can hold on to Your promise that I can be fully equipped for all this entails. I decree over my children right now that "I train them up in the way they should go, and when they are older they will not depart from it!"

In Jesus' Name, Amen

Part 2 of 2: Suckers and Shooters

A trap seizes him by the heel; a snare holds him fast. A noose is hidden for him on the ground; a trap lies in his path. (Job 18:9-10)

Flee the evil desires of youth, and pursue righteousness, faith, love and peace, along with those who call on the Lord out of a pure heart... Those who oppose him (who follows the Lord) he must gently instruct, in the hope that God will grant them repentance leading them to a knowledge of the truth and that they will come to their senses and escape from the trap/snare of the devil who has taken them captive to do his will. (2 Timothy 2:22, 25-26)

As you know, I have been working in the yard recently, specifically an area that had been untended, left "au natural" for a few years. Not only did the work of raking reveal "suckers" at the base of my growing trees which needed to be snipped for the health of the trees, but there were many times I nearly tripped and fell over the "shooters" too. Shooters are the wild vines that run across the yard, shooting from here to there in no particular pattern, periodically reconnecting and anchoring to the soil~ which is un-selective as to what it is willing to receive. As I was raking, clearing the next section, oftentimes my foot became entangled in a shooter. They were so strongly anchored that the vine didn't give way as my foot hit it, rather it held firm, forcing my foot to halt its forward motion unexpectedly. While I never landed on my tush, I did find it irritating and inconvenient, distracting me from the work, taking my focus off of what I wanted to accomplish. I constantly found myself bent over; yanking out the shooters, pulling them up in long sections, following them across the land, so no one else had opportunity to stumble in my yard.

Can you relate? Do you ever feel like you're going along fine in life when suddenly, from an unexpected source, you hit a wall, or have your forward progress stopped, or you "take a hit" that throws you off balance? John 10:10 warns us that the enemy is here only to steal, kill and destroy. He has no other mission but that. He loves areas of our lives that we allow to remain "untended" for a while~ areas where we "let things slide", or where we are overconfident and inattentive. He likes areas of little com-promises because they are subtle, seemingly unimportant.

It didn't take much space for the shooters to enter my yard. They snuck in, not all at once, but grew gradually under leaf-cover, unnoticed until I walked through~ then they reached out and grabbed at my ankles, knocking me off balance when I least expected it.

Let me give you some examples, for your own "self check-up". This isn't meant to be an exhaustive list, but you'll get the idea on some areas of entanglement that can knock you way off track with God: do you read horoscopes thinking they're harmless, not realizing they are a gateway to witchcraft that allow direct access of your home and children to the influence of demons, then wonder why the kids are so disrespectful and rebellious? What about "romance" novels~ do you allow your mind to wander in the vivid description of "lust scenes" and wonder why your boring spouse doesn't..., or imagining the scene with someone other than your spouse, then wonder why you find yourself dissatisfied and your marriage relationship shallow? What about the music you listen to: do find yourself singing along to song lyrics dishonoring to God- lyrics that snuck in casually but now come out of your mouth even though you never focused on learning them? Out of the abundance of the heart the mouth speaks.

Seemingly little compromises in areas of life you considered unimportant or insignificant can snag your feet as you attempt to live for God, robbing you of His Best as you settle for "just enough to get by" in this life. It is our job to be vigilant over our "yard" as we walk through this life. We are responsible for what we allow. We will stand before God and give account for every word, every choice. His desire is to empower us with the Holy Spirit to live triumphantly~ reaching down and pulling up by the root those shooters that entangle us or others connected with us, clearing the path for successfully reaching our designed destiny.

Victories that are not maintained must be re-fought and re-won, the shooters re-pulled. God is faithful to watch over His Word and to perform it as we expectantly speak it out. He is faithful to come along side and partner with us, with you! Any time this side of heaven is not too late! The longer we wait to clear the shooters, the more work it will be~ but it will still be so worth it!

Father God, Thank You for the opportunity to partner with You in this process of clearing the shooters from my life, that I don't have to "go it alone"! Help me to identify the shooters of compromise in my life so I don't just settle for good, but propel forward toward the best ordained destiny You have for me! Thank You that I can hold on to Your promise to be fully equipped for all this entails. I decree vigilance over my life right now, that as You and I partner, I will step into ALL that You have for me!

In Jesus' Name, Amen

Reality TV or a Real Covenant?

There is a friend who sticks closer than a brother. (Proverbs 18:24)

"Never will I leave you; never will I forsake you." So we say with confidence "The Lord is my Helper; I will not be afraid. What can man do to me?" (Hebrews 13:5b-6)

Have you ever had a friend let you down? Have you ever realized a particular relationship meant more to you than it did to the other person? If you have ever experienced a "boy-girl" break up, then you know one version of what I'm talking about! Unfortunately, these experiences aren't limited to middle school, are they? Sometimes the people who mean the most in our lives let us down, disappoint us and betray our trust sometimes unintentionally- but sometimes not. Regardless, it hurts.

In this day and age of "reality" TV shows and a society that actually glorifies backstabbing, deceit, deception and violating a trust or a confidence, how refreshing it is to know that we have One we can always count on! While people are imperfect and unpredictable, God remains constant. His love is unconditional. He is never farther away than our whispered call. He always answers. Jesus is "always always"!

You see, God made a covenant with us and sealed it in the blood of His only Son Jesus, Whose resurrection we recently celebrated. The value of that is usually lost on us Westerners, who are unfamiliar with the whole significance of blood covenant ritual. In short, once the partnership ceremony of the two people is complete they are bound to the terms of the covenant~ defending, protecting and fighting for each other until one or the other passes away from old age or in defense of the partner; pretty intense! Nothing at all like what we view on TV or lived through in middle school, is it?

So, in light of our current societal values, how would you feel knowing you had Someone Who would always back you up, always be there to defend you, encourage, support, protect, keep you straight and have your back~ Who was always there every time you called? If you have asked Jesus into your life, to be your Savior and Lord, then you've started in the right path to experience this!

Is there more available? You bet! That's just the first step...

Father God, I ask You to come into my heart right now, not
just to save me from sin, but also to be my Lord. I want that
Covenant Partnership with You, not just a "get out of hell"
card. Please show me what that partnership means as I begin
to trust and interact with You at a whole new level.

In Jesus' Name Amen

Do Whatever He Tells You

His mother said to the servants, "Do whatever He tells you." (John 2:5)

Does the Lord delight in burnt offerings and sacrifices as much as in obeying the Lord? To obey is better than sacrifice. (I Samuel 15:22a)

... love is the fulfillment of the law. (Romans 13:10b)

Jesus did His first miracle at His mother's request and officially launched His ministry. Mary, Jesus and His disciples attended a wedding and the host ran out of wine. To prevent embarrassment of their friends, she took matters into her own hands and explained to Jesus what had happened, then instructed the servants to "do whatever He tells you."

That same instruction still stands. In I Samuel, we see that obeying what God tells us to do is held in higher esteem than any sacrifice we can bring before the throne. Romans backs that up with the short but powerful statement that "Love is the fulfillment of the law." What a relief it must have been to those who loved God and sought after Him in that era!! Although we still deal with it now, we don't even comprehend how many nit-picky little rules and regulations the Jews of that day dealt with!

It was so bad, they had (and still have) a book called the Talmud, which is all the laws imposed upon the people by every priest who chose to add his two-cents to the book. There were laws about how far you could walk on the Sabbath, about how much you could carry on the Sabbath, etc. Today we call that legalism. There are many churches that expect us to comply with their rules on how long your hair should be, or how many committees you serve on, or how much volunteer time you put in to kids ministry, and so on. Another term for it is "works mentality"~ the idea that we have to do all these things, activities and meet these requirements, in order to be acceptable to God.

When Jesus walked the earth, He summed it up in this: we are to love and obey~ that's it! No volumes of rules and regulations to follow, only love God and show it by obeying what He says to do! How freeing!

Dr. Chuck Pierce, world-renown prophet and leadership covering of this ministry, tells the story from early in his years when he walked his yard one night and "had a talk with God". He wrote down on a paper all of his concerns, his struggles, the weights he was carrying, and held them up to God. He had a very frank discussion on where he was at~ he was totally honest with God. God's answer to that list was this: "go buy your wife a new dress for Easter"... NOT at all the answer he was expecting since he had very little in the bank, barely enough for a dress, and that was one of his concerns!! God told him that if he was faithful in that One Thing, in other words if he obeyed, God would handle the rest. Because he loved and trusted God, he did obey, and within a few short months, every single thing that had weighed Dr. Pierce down was taken care of, including his wife's physical healing!

In my life I have seen pieces fall into place like dominoes because I trusted and obeyed God. Recently I faced a crossroads that my mind didn't understand, but because my heart was full of His peace I moved forward. I am now are reaping the blessings that follow obedience!

The good news is that God is the same: yesterday, today and forever. Along with that, He is no respecter of persons: what He does for one of us, He will do for any of us! The call still goes out today: do whatever He tells you! Are you obeying what He says, or are you so busy doing "good things" that you don't have time to do "the best thing" and obey His personal instruction to you? The most powerful way we express our love to God is in obeying what He tells us to do. It's more important to obey Him than to sacrifice our time in activities of doing things for Him instead.

So what is He asking of you? Spend time with Him. Hear His voice, then obey whatever He tells you to do!

Father God, I choose to listen to You and hear Your voice! I want to do what You want me to do. I want to obey You and let You change my life!

In Jesus' Name, Amen!

Moving Into the New

For everything there is a season. (Ecclesiastes 3:1)

For we are God's workmanship, created in Christ Jesus to do good works, which God prepared in advance for us to do. (Ephesians 2:10)

As I write this, I'm back out on my deck, in the sun, with a hot cup of blueberry tea. My puppy sits not far away, in the grass, on guard as she watches for any intruding squirrels or geese that may need to be chased. The various birds are calling back and forth to each other, the sky is an amazing shade of blue, and the clouds are soft wisps puffing by my section of sky... again.

Our season has changed. The lake is no longer covered with a thick layer of ice strong enough to hold die hard fishermen. In this new season out will come the fishing boats. In this new season, our girls will run down the hill onto the beach with toys to create a sand castle, or grab sticks to throw into the lightly rippling water for our happily waiting puppy to retrieve from the still-chilly water. Yes, the season has changed.

When it comes to weather, we in Michigan expect many changes. While we may enjoy some of the changes more than others, they don't surprise us~ we just roll with it. However when it comes to the ending of a job, or a friendship, or some era in our life, it can be a much different story, can't it? My kids don't need me to change their diapers anymore. They dress themselves, run and play, and spend the night at a friend's house. They still fit on my lap, although they hang over the edges of my legs more than ever before. Someday they will be the Moms cradling their little ones and giving angel kisses at bedtime. My hair used to stay a golden blonde on its own; now it needs some assistance. My grill used to get much use with a certain group of people gathered on our deck or in the yard, but seasons change, people move, new activities claim time in the schedule and the familiar gives way to the new~ even without our permission.

The good news is that God moves with us into that new season! He didn't stay in the old and send us on our way alone. God comes along~ in fact He's been here waiting for us to arrive, having prepared the new to meet us. God is not limited by time and space as we are. We are designed to live in the present~ not the past which created fond memories of yesteryear, nor the future with it's potential changes, challenges, and joys, but in the present: right here and right now.

Today is a gift~ open it and live it to the full! Yes, our seasons will change again, but for now we have today. Let's not wish for snow, or the changing colors of fall when for the first time in months the thermometer finally hit sixty! Let's live today, with all the treasures and special moments it holds. Remember: they are each "once-in-a- lifetime"!

Dear God, thank you that You move with me into the new. I
can both celebrate and grieve the coming and going of each
life season with You by my side, never alone. Help me to
live today in the place where You are present~ here.

In Jesus' Name, Amen

Ever Been Betrayed?

...Peter stood up and said "...Judas, who served as a guide for those who
arrested Jesus- he was one of our number and shared in this ministry...
it is necessary to choose one of the men who have been with us the
whole time... {to} take over this apostolic ministry." (Acts 1:15-21)

Ever been betrayed? We know Jesus was for sure, but have you ever
thought about the disciples and how they felt? Jesus knew Judas' betrayal
was coming. In fact, He sweat blood drops in anticipation of the whole
event, but the disciples were clueless! It took them completely off guard
to have Judas betray Jesus~ and the rest of them! Can you imagine their
shock and horror? Their anger and helplessness? The natural tendency
would be to close up and not let anyone else "in" after that. On our own,
that really is the natural choice, but as we see from Peter's proposal to
the ministry team, God empowered him to "open back up", not let this
knife-in-the-heart stop them, fill the position with God's candidate and
proceed on schedule with The Mission. In the face of betrayal, they chose
to overcome natural self-preservation tendencies with fresh vulnerability.

How "God" is that?? It certainly isn't our natural human inclination!

Their Mission was bigger than them; they had a definite sense of
urgency and passion that couldn't be stopped! They surrendered their

damaged, betrayed human emotions to God's mighty hand and overcame any urge to isolate themselves by acting in faith to fill the leadership vacancy in the ministry. Wow! That's the epitome of "Get Over and On With It!"

We each have faced loss of relationship with at least one person in our lifetimes. I know that for me, to lose a church/ ministry partner or leader has always been the hardest for me to overcome and be willing to re-fill. My sense of expectation of them is higher than it is for those who don't even profess to know Jesus, so when backstabbing or deceit gets uncovered, I feel stupid for trusting them, and the last thing I want to do is to become vulnerable and open up to someone new right away.

I'm not alone in this either, am I? Look at the results in churches or ministries who experience lack of integrity by the leader in some area that becomes public. Those are tough shoes to fill, and the healing process can be made complicated for those who come in to help by the personal protective measures the hurt members take. Yet that's not God's best for any of us! He wants us to be completely vulnerable with Him, but wise in our choices of the people to whom we reveal our hearts. The enemy would love nothing more than to come in and isolate us from the rest of the Body who can be trusted and want to help us heal. The enemy is a master at division!

Take a look now at Jesus' words in John 15, especially verse 17: This is My command: Love Each Other.

He talks about joy, also. We, as His Body need to allow His grace to heal our hurts, for His love to come in, to stand in unity, and care for each other... and from today's verse: to then get up and "git after it!" Go forward, receive the new partner/leaders God brings our way. Move ahead with His unchanging Mission to share His love and His Gift of Jesus with everyone!

Father God, give me the grace to surrender my hurts to You, to receive those whom You bring to fill the void, and move forward with Your Mission at the forefront of my mind and heart.

In Jesus' Name, Amen

Already Prepared!

See, I am sending an angel ahead of you to guard you along the way
and to bring you to the place I have prepared. (Exodus 23:20)

This verse jumped off the page at me this week when I read this chapter as part of a prayer focus I'm doing from Dr. Chuck Pierce. I needed God's rhema Word for me right then, and this is the verse that He lit up.

A "Rhema word" is a verse or section of God's Word that we take to heart for our need at the moment. You see, His Word is universal, and always true, yet it becomes very personal when we listen, letting Him guide us through His Word to the spot with the promise we need for that moment. He knows exactly what we need and He knows where in the Bible the promise is. He also knows how to lead us to get us there. Our part is to listen, be obedient, and look with open eyes.

The nuggets I got out of this verse: God has protection assigned for me. God has sent me help and provision. I will make it because not only is He leading me, but He has already been to my future and has my place prepared, which means He expects me to make it there! It doesn't mean I will enjoy all details of the journey~ life can be hard~ but it does mean that as I choose to trust Him, moment by moment, I get closer to my destination and all that I will need is available before I ask. You see, He always starts with the end in mind!

> *Father, God, Daddy, thank You for Your rhema word! Thank*
> *You that You never change~ so You always provide, lead, guide,*
> *and protect. I know I can trust You in every area of life.*
>
> *In Jesus' Name, Amen*

Pedal Faster!

*Do not stop gathering together, as some are in the habit
of doing, but encourage one another, and especially more
as you see The Day approaching. (Hebrews 10:25)*

For He Himself is our peace. (Ephesians 2:14)

I've altered my exercise plan recently. With the onset of warmer
weather, I'm borrowing my daughter's mountain bike and zipping (or
chugging) along! Today was beautiful! The air was calm though cool, the
sky an emerging robin's egg blue as the chorus of birds cheered on the
sunrise. The roads were quiet as the earth was awakening to a new day.

I noticed something that connected in my spirit and I had to share
it with you. It gets harder to pedal as I come up to a knoll. It becomes
easier if I switch gears, quickening my pace on the approach. Otherwise
I feel like I'll get stuck part way up, and that would not be good... on so
many levels!

Jesus warned us about these last days, with wars, rumors of wars,
earthquakes, etc. We have recently had our share of these, and the prophets agree: they won't end anytime soon. They are a part of God's plan to
wake up the people of the earth who are lost, to get their attention so they

turn to Him before it is too late.

It's now our turn for a wake up call: the world needs to hear the good news of God's eternal love for them! They need to hear that it is His will to walk alongside them through their lives and stop the destroyer from taking them under. We need to speak up and let Him love them through us! It's time for us to speed up as we approach the "knoll". We need to pedal faster until we feel the burn in our thighs. We need to shift gears and focus in, determined to stand fast in the midst of chaos, letting God display His peace through us. We, His Body, standing united to each do our part with the gifts we have received, can make a huge difference in this ol' world we live in!

People are in fear and turmoil, but God's love is more powerful, which allows others to be drawn to us like a lighthouse shining through the storm of economic turbulence and the groanings of nature. He is our peace first. We hold fast to Him~ our God, our shield, our defender. Then we can share that peace with others.

Amen!

> *Father God, be my peace. Show me how to hold tightly to*
> *You! I see The Day approaching, and need Your power to*
> *"pedal faster", to "downshift" to the next gear so together*
> *we can reach this world, bringing them to safety!*

> *In Jesus' Name, Amen*

Down Payment on Perfection

For the wages of sin is death but the gift of God is eter-
nal life through Jesus Christ our Lord. (Romans 6:23)

We know that the whole creation has been groaning as in the pains of
childbirth right up to this present time. Not only so but we ourselves, who
have the first fruits of the Spirit, groan inwardly as we wait eagerly for
our adoption as sons, the redemption of our bodies. (Romans 8:22-23)

All the earth shall worship You And sing praises to You; They
shall sing praises to Your Name. Selah (Psalm 66:4)

Our life~ so easy to take for granted. We're so used to the sights and
sounds around us in our work-a-day life. When we go on vacation it's
like we look at our world through new eyes.

This week I'm living a dream: we're vacationing in Hawaii, my first
time here! I'm blown away by the sights, sounds and smells. In fact,
during my first twenty-four hours here I kept asking: "If Hawaii is this
beautiful, what must the Garden of Eden have been like??" That thought
boggles my mind! People have lived here on planet earth for two thou-

sand years now, and sin has caused creation to groan and fade under its weight. What must Eden have looked like when it was young, fresh clean and vibrant, unstained? What I see this week is but a pale comparison of original design.

As I walk through the island, I hear the calls of tropical birds, making musical patterns I haven't before heard. The brooks, streams and waterfalls gurgle babbling praise to their Creator, the ocean thunders thanks from its depths~ a deep voice that rhythmically crashes onto the shore. The flowers and fauna stretch toward the sun to offer their brilliant colors an offering wholly and acceptably pleasing to the One Who gave them such a gift. All of nature in unison!

Are we so thankful as they? Not only do we have this natural life, but God has given us His most splendid gift of eternal life through His Son! We are given the opportunity to be by His side forever and ever~ not passively sitting on white puffy clouds with harps, but we get to experience the power and glory of His majestic splendor! He will crown us with our rewards and provide for us our mansions!

Here on earth the Holy Spirit, the third person of the Trinity or Godhead, is our down-payment, our deposit securing the fullness of our future life with God. He plans for us to begin to live as His children, exercising our dominion over creation in the "here and now" - not just the "hereafter". Later, in the real Paradise, we will receive our crowns and the fullness of our reward, but we can walk assured of them here and now, experiencing victory over the obstacles in this life.

Father God, I choose to walk in thankfulness this day, for all You have given to provide for my needs. I choose to see the beauty that surrounds me even in familiar surroundings, and to set my sights on the fact that these are just a down-payment, a foreshadowing, of the coming beauty and fulfillment I will experience as I walk hand in hand with You.

Thank You for giving the ultimate gift~ Jesus Christ, to provide me with an eternal life of perfection when we see each other face to face.

In Jesus' Name, Amen

The Life is in the Seed!

He is like a tree planted by streams of water, which
yields its fruit in season & whose leaf does not wither.
Whatever he does prospers. (Psalm 1:3)

But the one who received the seed that fell on good soil is the man
who hears the Word and understands it. He produces a crop yielding
a hundred, sixty or thirty times what was sown. (Matthew 13:23)

I had the pleasure of spending a considerable chunk of my morning planting our family garden with a family member. He made the rows, I planted to seeds, then he covered them; together we worked, side by side. As I worked, I kept hearing God whisper to me: "The life is in the seed, the life is in the seed!"

How true it is! This year's seed was a part of last year's harvest. Each little kernel of corn I planted held within it the potential for a full stalk of new corn, yielding as many as four to six ears each of fresh sweet corn. The life was definitely in the seed. Without the planting of the seed today there could be no future harvest: no gathering arm loads in the summer, no fresh-frozen corn to enjoy throughout the fall and into the winter.

The seeds didn't look "alive": they weren't sprouting, they weren't pretty, there was nothing special that drew attention to them, but I trusted the instructions that I was given. Soak them overnight, plant them six-to-eight inches apart, in a row, water them, weed them, and they will not only sprout, but produce the harvest of corn I desire. I knew once we covered them, we would never see them in that form again because an underground transformation would take place...

How like our lives! God the Father is our Master Gardener Who desires His life to transform our "kernel" into a productive "stalk" with an abundant "crop". He cares for us, planting us in a sphere where He intends us to bring His influence and harvest. Soaking is our salvation in Christ. Our water is His Word, our sunlight~ His love. When the cares of this world attempt to choke us, He weeds the garden and allows us to breathe again as we "cast our cares on Him".

The seeds didn't complain about where I planted them, which row they were in, or what seed they were next to. They received the water and sunshine without question. They won't protest when we pull the life-draining weeds from close proximity to their tender shoots. They won't even fuss about the transformation from hard kernel to green stalks. They release their existence as seed to be transformed into conduits of life for a new crop: tall stalks with kernels and ears that will fill many mouths during multiple meals- how drastically different than the single kernel of today!

The life is in the seed! His life is in you and me! He is the Master Gardener; we will do well to partner with Him. His desire is to transform us into His likeness, using us as the conduits of love and power to a whole other "crop" of people reached for salvation in Christ!

Father God, display Yourself as my Personal Master Gardener: cause that exciting transformation of who I am today into who You see I can be tomorrow! Give me eyes to see who needs me to be Your conduit of love and power today, and the obedience to do exactly what You ask me to do. Lord, I desire to produce a "bumper crop" of love for You!

In Jesus' Name, Amen

Mobile Connections

He existed before all things and in Him all things
hold together... (Colossians 1:17)

I recently read a popular book, or should I say I experienced a book, called *The Shack*, by William P. Young. It's absolutely amazing! It questions religious legalism and expands the view most mainstream Christians hold of Jesus in His power, all while the main character spends time with God (known in the book as Papa) and receives a deep internal healing from the most horrendous wound in his life. A profound masterpiece!

Following is a brief excerpt from one of their conversations that pertains to today's verse and picks up mid-conversation in a discussion of priorities; italics are mine...

"'If you put God at the top, what does that really mean and how much is enough? How much time do you give me before you can go on about the rest of your day, the part that interests you so much more?"

Papa again interrupted. "You see, Mackenzie, I don't just want a piece of you and a piece of your life. Even if you were able, which you are not, to give me the biggest piece, that is not what I want. I want all of you and all of every part of you and your day."

Now Jesus spoke again. "Mack, I don't want to be first among a list of values; I want to be at the center of everything. When I live in you, then together we can live through everything that happens to you. Rather than a pyramid, I want to be at the center of a mobile, where everything in your life- your friends, family, occupation, thoughts, activities- is connected to me but moves with the wind, in and out and back and forth, in an incredible dance of being.'"

Isn't that a cool picture? Can't you just imagine a mobile blowing back and forth, dipping and swaying in the fresh spring breeze of the Holy Spirit? The center-point is Jesus, and the objects on the mobile represent the various pieces of your life. All parts of you are connected to Him, He feels every vibration in any segment of your mobile. He is tuned in to everything about you!

Contrast that with a stone pyramid. It's built with layer upon massive layer. Solid and unyielding, the top point cannot blend with the next layer. While the levels are united to make one object, say one life, there is no connection between the differing segments. The blocks of stone are compartmentalized. To fit God into that structure, He would be limited to one block~ or even if He had several, He wouldn't be impacting all, as there's no flow between the parts. Where does He fit in your life? Do you dance with Him or rigidly define His place in your life? Ponder that today...

Father God, Papa, I want You to impact everything in my
life! I hold nothing back from You! Be my center-point. I
want to share the incredible dance of being with You!

In Jesus' Name, Amen

Marching Orders: Part 1

Then Jesus came to them and said 'ALL authority in heaven and earth has been given to Me. Therefore go and make disciples of all nations, baptizing them in the Name of the Father and of the Son and of the Holy Spirit, and teaching them to obey everything I have commanded you, And surely I will be with you always, to the very end of the age.' (Matthew 28:18-20)

With this week holding the special remembrance of Memorial Day, I first want to say a huge THANK YOU to all the veterans, current military and their families! Because of your great sacrifices, we enjoy greater freedoms than any other country in the world, and we don't take that lightly.

My Grandpa was in the Navy during World War II. Even though he had young twin daughters and his third child was on her way, he accepted his marching orders, fulfilled his duty to his country, and came home to meet that newest child, who was then age two. He took each of his responsibilities seriously.

Do you?

What I mean is, we as Christians also have our "marching orders" and a duty to fulfill to our Commander in Chief, just as my Grandpa had a duty to his country. Yes, God heals the brokenhearted, and establishes us in righteousness, but then He also commissions us into His service. Salvation isn't just a "get out of hell free" card where we ask Jesus into our hearts then sit back, eating bonbons and continue to live the way we had before meeting Him. Christianity, not religion, is about relationship with the King of the Universe, about being confirmed to His likeness, filled with the Holy Spirit, and empowered to share His love with everyone around us, which will shake the gates of hell and free the people God loves so much! We are a people on a mission! We are made to bring Him praise~ not just us voicing our praise to Him, but also others praising God because of the transformational work they see going on inside of us which spills out and overflows from us into the streets on which we live!

So I ask again: do you take your responsibility seriously? Just as in WWII then, now lives, futures, countries and communities hang in the balance of eternity. Will you tell those in your path what Jesus means to you? Will your life bring praise from them to your Commander in Chief, High King Jesus? Is your life becoming a Memorial to the One Who loves you most of all? I challenge you to do so!

Dear King of my heart, I choose to follow Your commands, to let You love others through me, and to touch lives for eternity. May I bring high praise to You because I honor You and take my responsibility seriously.

In Jesus' Name, Amen

Marching Orders: Part 2

Do not conform any longer to the pattern of this world,
but be transformed by the renewing of your mind. Then
you will be able to test and approve what God's will is~
His good, pleasing and perfect will. (Romans 12:2)

parable of the Rich Young Ruler (Matthew 19:16-22)

Continuing on the previous theme, I want to stay on the idea of "marching orders". You see, there are two different types of marching orders that we receive in our Christian life, just as there are in military life. Keeping them straight will help us in our own personal walk. It's no fun to find ourselves in "frustration mode" because we tried to implement orders God gave, only to realize they were specifically for someone else~ not us, and we have these two mixed up.

First of all, we have our "general orders". These encompass things meant for ALL Christians, so items like the Ten Commandments, the Beatitudes, and the Great Commission, and the Love Walk. These apply to us all without exception. Knowing these makes our decision-making process on choices we face much more simple: we don't have to think about whether or not it's okay to steal, lie to our boss, or have sex outside of marriage, or forgive a back-stabber because the Bible is very clear on God's standards for these issues. Most people have a greater understanding of these "general orders" than they do of the "specific orders" because they are more visible and more readily discussed from a church pulpit due to their all-encompassing nature. The second is more obscure and personal...

The concept of personal orders is like that when, in the military, a General will say to a Private, "go take these papers over there" or "you are on KP duty today" or "we need extra reinforcement over here in this high stress area so go report for duty". These specific orders are not for every Private under that General, but only for the one he specifically addresses. In the same way there are things God tells us personally, but may not tell our next door neighbor or best friend. One Christian leader I know described God's specific orders to him as "others may... you cannot". And he obeyed "because God said so". This is a similar concept to "God's Rhema Word" for you, where the Holy Spirit lights up a passage or a concept as you are reading your Bible, praying or hearing a message, and it's exactly what you needed for direction or encouragement at that moment of that specific situation.

One area where we see God giving specific marching orders is in the story of the Rich Young Ruler. We see in this story that the man was young, probably late teens or early twenties at most. He was a ruler, so he was very high profile and influential in his hometown. And he was rich. When he came to question Jesus, Jesus did as was so typical of Him: He asked questions of the man. This young man actually told Jesus that he had kept every law perfectly!! Wow! (Do you know anyone who has kept all Ten Commandment not only with their actions but also with their words and thoughts?? Neither do I, but that's what this guy told Jesus.) The Bible tells us that Jesus "looked at him and loved him". He didn't get mad and call him a liar even though He could see right through the façade. Jesus gave him an opportunity to demonstrate Commandment #1: You shall have no other gods before you, by asking him to go sell all he had and give to the poor. Jesus gave him a personal, specific order here for the sole purpose of exposing the truth about what/who truly was this man's god: his possessions, or Father God?

We know what he chose~ he rejected his specific marching orders in favor of what he loved more than God. It's very possible that had the man said "Sure, I'm on it right now" that Jesus would have said "No, it's okay: now I know where your heart is!" but unfortunately it didn't end that way.

There are times God asks us to let go of certain things or people in our lives, but these are for specific marching order purpose: to create something new in our lives/character or to spare us from something that He, in His Sovereignty, sees ahead on our current path.

Jesus isn't afraid of you being wealthy~ He had a personal treasurer for His ministry, and it was so common for Him to give that no one thought anything about it when Judas got up and left in the middle of Passover dinner: they thought he was going to give to the poor again. The fact is that God wants you to have wealth, but not for wealth to have you. For His Kingdom to prosper, for us to accomplish all He intends for us to, we must have financial resources to be empowered and to empower those around us~ not only do we need the finances but He needs to be able to move those through us into the hands of others as well.

I have a dear friend who received a specific marching order just recently: God asked her to give up a valuable painting worth thousands of dollars to someone she hardly knew. Because she was faithful to do it, she had an open spot on her wall when, a couple weeks later God provided her a new painting that is a visual representation of the ministry He is bringing into her life! Had she not obeyed, chances are at best she wouldn't have had a place for the new painting. At worst she would not have gotten the new one, which is now a constant reminder for her of God's direct action in her life! She has set the precedent of willingness to obey God's specific marching orders, so now he knows He can trust her for greater orders.

How do we know His specific marching orders? Seek His presence in worship, not just the blessings from His hands. Look for His face. Spend time with Him so your mind is transformed, as the above verse says, then you will know not just your general orders, but His specific, good, pleasing and perfect will!

Now, go be a God-chaser and change your world!

Dear King of my heart, I worship You and seek Your face, not just the blessings from Your hands. I listen to Your Word so I can be transformed and obey You to fulfill my specific marching orders. Today I live in the center of Your perfect will!

In Jesus' Name, Amen

Out of the Spider's Web

You shall know the truth and the truth shall set you free! *(John 8:32)*

Finding a new church these days can be a pretty interesting venture. Some have loud music for a young crowd, others prefer a quiet piano for the more traditional group. The sign in the front of the yard gives you an indication of the "lean" of their theology, but no information on the level of warmth to newcomers. Unfortunately, many churches are totally fine with where their memberships stand and where the boundaries of their friendship circles lie. Some look at you pretty funny if you come for a visit and inadvertently take "their" seat, but others are warm and welcoming.

I have a dear friend who was sooo hungry to go deeper with God and connect in a local body again that she jumped right away when, as they visited a church for the first time, a friendly someone invited them to join the upcoming Bible study the church was hosting. After a couple weeks of getting into it (and we're talking "heavy immersion" of four nights a week right off the bat) her spirit was unsettled when they attended. She and her husband dug in deep to the Word on their own and asked more and more questions in class on what they were reading in the Bible but were pushed aside as the leader continued with his own agenda, even when it was "question and answer time". Their children also felt unsettled with one significantly acting out, we believe, because of the danger he felt within his spirit. Finally our friends asked some questions of me on some things that weren't being answered within their Bible Study time.

As I asked more questions to get a clearer picture of what they were facing, I began my own research, discovering that this was a cult masquerading as a Christian church~ and not just any church, but claiming to be THE Remnant Church of the book of Revelation! Further discussion with my friend and her husband revealed that they had found some theological errors on their own because of the initiative they had taken to get to know the Word of God. God guided this process by "highlighting" verses on which they needed to raise questions. Truth became revealed as the "Bible study leaders" refused to answer them, or in some cases replied with "well that verse really doesn't mean what it says, and we wrote a whole book that explains what that verse is really supposed to mean". Scary stuff!

Why do I share this story with you? Because my friends were fortunate: they know the voice of God in their spirits, and with some input from us on the outside of that "spider web" were able to say: "no, this is what the Bible says in context." Not everyone exposed to this web of lies makes it back out and onto the right track. You see, either the Bible is the inspired Word of God or it's not. No gray area here~ yes or no. If the Bible in context is said to have error, then which part is wrong? Do we get to pick and choose what to keep and what to toss? Either the Bible is absolute, or it is irrelevant. God's Word is a lamp to our feet and a light to our path. It is sharper than any two- edged sword, able to distinguish between bone and marrow, soul and spirit. It is Truth. It will set our hearts free!

I'm happy to report my dear friends are safe and deeper in their faith now. They are connected in a healthy church~ I didn't say perfect, but healthy. The Holy Spirit guarded them and prompted their questions;

now they know His voice more clearly than ever. They held to Truth more tightly than their desire to be included in a new church family, or the opinions of "nice people". They trusted God to light their path, allowing Him to re-direct them and used us to help confirm that process. They are growing and they are free!

My desire is that you are equipped to handle this type of thing too, because you will face deception in one form or another in this world. The closer we get to the End, the more difficult it will be to determine Truth from lies. You are valuable, God's truth will set you free. When you face a situation that needs to be questioned, I want you to be able to stand against it, hold on to your freedom, and have the same outcome as my other dear friends.

To help drive this home, I'm going to give you 1 Corinthians 16:13-14 from three different versions; one of them is bound to speak to you.

*Be on your guard; stand firm in the faith; be wo/men of courage; be strong. Do everything in love.

*Watch, stand fast in the faith, be brave, be strong. Let all that you do be done with love.

*Keep your eyes open, hold tight to your convictions, give it all you've got, be resolute, and love without stopping.

Father God, thank You for the Truth in Your Word that sets us free! May I submit to Your leading and hold tightly to my convictions from You that I may not be led astray. The days are evil, but You are holy and just. Keep me on alert so I can lovingly help others hold fast as well.

In Jesus' Name, Amen

Mosquitoes or Fruit?

*You will seek Me and find Me when you seek Me
with all your heart. (Jeremiah 29:13)*

Sometimes finding what we're looking for is easier than others, isn't it? I was reminded of this yesterday as I weeded the garden while our daughters picked black raspberries in the bushes nearby. I had scooped out the situation and pointed out the bushes with "the mother load" to make it easier on the girls.

You know, black raspberries aren't the easiest of all berries to collect. The girls wore long pants and zip up jackets with long sleeves to keep the mosquitoes and prickers off their delicate skin. This particular morning, our youngest was more focused on finding the distractions than the berries, and several times I had to leave my chore to redirect her. Once her Mamma was nearby, her focus returned and she was well-able to locate the large juicy berries dangling from the bushes in front of her.

It's like that when we look for God sometimes, too, isn't it? We get lost looking at the prickers and swatting at mosquitoes instead of the ripe fruit from the Vine right in front of us. That's how the enemy of our soul wants to keep us: too distracted to absorb The Word and hear The Voice. The good news is: He promises that we will find Him when we seek after

Him with our whole heart. The Holy Spirit gently redirects our attention when we let Him, and the rewards are both immediate and eternal!

You want to find God? Seek Him with your whole heart. After all, a promise is a promise!

> *Father God, I want to find You. Please forgive my distractions and redirect me back to You. I know You have my best at heart, and have provided for me what I need; I just need to look and listen to find it and see You right in front of me!*
>
> *In Jesus' Name, Amen*

Indeed!

He whom the Son sets free is free indeed! (John 8:36)

Okay, so "indeed" is not a word we use a lot in our culture, but it is an important word in this verse, so let's look at *The Message* and *The Amplified* versions to see what else we can learn and dig out of this one-liner. *The Message* says "So if the Son sets you free, you are free through and through." Very cool, okay, now *The Amplified* words it this way "So if the Son liberates you (makes you free men) then you are really and unquestionably free." Hmm, those words don't leave much room for second-guessing the completeness of our freedom, do they? There's no gray area where we could misinterpret this to mean partially free or somewhat free, or free in certain areas of life only. This is real, thorough, complete freedom!

God paid the highest price for our freedom: blood had to be shed to secure the "pardon papers" from hell for us, which is exactly what Jesus did! When we accepted the price He paid, received His life and forgiveness, we "picked up those pardon papers", and walked out into the light of a new life that was unlike anything else we had known before!

"Cool! So now I am free~ let's throw out the Ten Commandments and everything is legal!" ...well, that's not exactly what I meant! Yes, we can do whatever we want... God only asks that we show our thankfulness for Jesus paying our penalty by living a life with only one rule, His only rule~ not man's multitude of rules, but His Law of Love. We are to owe no man anything, except the debt of love.

Paul dealt with this issue of freedom. He said "all things are legal, but not all things are beneficial". For example, I was free in my relationship with my former spouse. He trusted me to not lie to him. If I had, I would have damaged the trust between us and we would have experienced less intimacy in our relationship. Because I valued our relationship, I choose not to lie, even though I was 'free' to do so.

The other facet of freedom is that God desires our best, for us to walk through this life unhindered from the garbage that entangles people in this world, the heaviness that weighs people down and causes them sickness, stress, early death, and leaves their destinies unfulfilled. We have the ability to choose how much of His freedom we experience in this life! It's all laid out in front of us, like the food at Old Country Buffet. The choice is ours as to how much of God's goodness and freedom we choose to access, to put on our plate and taste, so to speak. I want His emotional freedom: He resolves the bad experiences and heals. I want His physical freedom: He literally heals and renews my body. I want His spiritual freedom: He removes the enemy strongholds and curses, then cleans out the "yucky residue" left behind from my time in the world.

How much of God's freedom do you want to experience in your life? Have you asked Him for it? He has made provision for you to receive it!

Father God, Daddy, thank You for Your gift of freedom! I ask
for Your wisdom to use it rightly. Lord, I need to experience a
new level of freedom in the area of ... in order to fulfill my des-

tiny. Please meet me in this area so I can receive Your strategy!

In Jesus' Name, Amen

Wait and Stand

But they that wait upon the Lord shall renew their strength.
They shall mount up with wings as eagles, they shall run and
not grow weary, they shall walk and not faint. (Isaiah 40:31)

This past week, my girls picked out a poster for me at the Christian bookstore in town. It has this verse overlaid on a beautiful sunset of blues fading to shades of gold, and as you may guess, two eagles soaring above all the rest of the life that we can imagine below. It came at just the right time...

I recently faced an important personal decision with many ramifications and secondary decisions that followed. In short it flipped my world upside down. I knew I had done the right thing to obey God and stand, but not everyone agreed with my choice. God had told me to stand and watch what He would do, but in the time window of twelve hours prior to my girls picking out this poster I had been challenged by others to do more than "just stand and watch". I had the power to act, to defend my point of view, to force others to hear my side. I had "the goods" on the others involved. Yet to "lay out the cards" I held would have been to turn my back on what I had been called to. To act on my own would have been to "un-surrender" it to God.

Do you know when we face the most temptation? When we have the power of choice: even if we think of a plan of action in the midst of a given circumstance, if we lack the ability to carry it through, it's not a temptation. It's moments like this particular one I had, when the power to react is well within our grasp that we have the real choice to make.

So my girls gave me this poster, not realizing that God had given me a Rhema word months before "to stand against what was coming and see Him work", in other words "to wait on Him" and here they were confirming His Word to me at just the right moment. How like God is that?? He uses whatever means He has available to confirm His word, to encourage us and keep us on track. I had been praying about how to respond in the hours before receiving it (I wondered: had the season for waiting now passed, and this was a time of action, finally?), and He used my girls to remind me of His promise and His directions to me through a poster!

The poster now hangs in a prominent place in our home, as a beautiful and timely reminder from God for this season in our lives. Someday the girls may have a greater understanding of its significance and timing, but for the moment all they really understand is that their gift made Mommy's eyes leak happy tears. I resurrendered my choice and the emotions that came with it to God's mighty hand, and I was renewed to stand and wait on our all- knowing, ever present, all mighty Father God to sort through it all and lead by His strong and gentle hand.

Father God, thank You for Your faithfulness and the way You renew Your words and directions to my heart when I stop long enough to listen to You! Thank You for knowing the end from the beginning, and that no circumstance is too big for You!

In Jesus' Name, Amen

Middle School Friends

For God so loved the world He gave His only begotten Son, that whoso-ever believes in Him shall not perish but have everlasting life. (John 3:16)

Recently my daughter has been going through some friend troubles. She has been trying to find that one true friend she can trust with all her heart; looking for a friend she can see, knowing it might take awhile for that. So for now she's chosen God.

These past few weeks the youth group has been talking about the Love of God, trying to describe how much God loves us. She said 'the story that I believe touched everyone in the youth group the most was the story of Abraham and Isaac. God told Abraham to sacrifice Isaac, his only son. Abraham could have argued with God and said that he didn't want to and that God was crazy or insane. No, Abraham listened and trusted God. He knew God would come through. So the story finishes with an angel coming to Abraham, right before he killed his son, saying "Don't harm him, you have showed Me that you are obedient.'"

We really have no idea what it must have been like for Abraham to have to hear that he was supposed to sacrifice his only son, for whom he had waited twenty-five years. "It must have been immensely hard for him." Then she continued "I imagined how God must have felt when He sent His Son to earth to save us. God loved us soooo much that He gave His Son for us!!"

"The leader said, "Think of one person right now who, if anyone tried to hurt them or bully them, you couldn't stand it. You would punch anyone who dared to hurt your person. Now imagine having to sacrifice that person like Abraham and Isaac. Would you obey or would you protest? The way you feel about your person is how God feels toward us. His love is soooo great we can't even comprehend it. It just blows us away."

"After class we had time where we could just talk to God. He spoke to me and said, 'Just as Abraham had to wait at least twenty-five years for Isaac, so you will have to wait for your true friend.'" She said, "Mom, those words just hit me in the face. It gets even better though; I heard God say 'While you wait for this friend, come to Me and I will listen. I will understand better than anyone else ever could. Trust Me and I won't ever let you down.'"

"Mom, how about them apples?! If someone feels desperate for a friend, boyfriend, girlfriend etc, I think they should go to God. He will be the Best Friend while He is preparing her 'perfect match'. People need to be able to talk to Him about anything before they can talk to a true friend. If they make Him Number One in life He will bless them with that true friend. We all need to feel His love before anyone else's and then we will never be desperate or lonely again!"

Wise words from such a young lady! They did a Momma's heart good! I pray you take the lesson from her words to heart, and have conversations like this in your home also!

Dear Father, please help me to understand Your love and feel the pure-
ness of it. Help me to know that even if I have to wait awhile for my
true friend You will always be there. Let me feel Your love and be able
to share it with others. Help me to know that You will comfort me

when I feel lonely and dance with me when I'm happy. Thank You

In Jesus' Name, Amen

Canning Beans

Then David said to Saul, "Let no man's heart fail because of him;
your servant will go and fight with this Philistine."... So it was, when
the Philistine arose and came and drew near to meet David, that
David hurried and ran toward the army to meet the Philistine. Then
David put his hand in his bag and took out a stone; and he slung it
and struck the Philistine in his forehead so that the stone sank into his
forehead, and he fell on his face to the earth. (1Samuel 17:32-50)

Last week my girls joined me in canning beans from our garden for the first time. Here is what came out of conversation as we worked...

Canning beans is a whole lot like our lives. We get filled with the Holy Spirit but when the time comes to let our light shine to others we "can" ourselves~ put ourselves in a jar. It can be for many reasons but the main reason is because we are afraid.

One daughter said "I know this out of my own experience. I was afraid to let my light shine. Then I realized two things. The first one is that God could help me break out of the jar that I put myself in. The second is that I should not be afraid of what people think of me when I shine my light for God. It was amazing when God helped me out of the jar. He led me to pray for a friend and gave me a prophetic word for her as well. When

I trusted God, came out of the "canning jar" and was obedient, the result was I helped a person in need! My friend was so thankful when I told her what God had said to me, because it was exactly what she needed. He knew it and let me give her the message!"

He can use you too; will you break out of the jar?

> *Dear Father, please help me to break out of my jar so that I may be used for Your works and Your works only. Help me to understand that even though I may be small or I may be one person, with Your help I can do great things.*
>
> *In Jesus' Name, Amen*

Joy!

Do not grieve, for the joy of the Lord is your strength. (Nehemiah 8:10)

*Restore to me the joy of Your salvation and grant to me
a willing spirit, to sustain me. (Psalm 51:12)*

*You have made known to me the path of life; You will fill me with joy in
Your presence, with eternal pleasure at Your right hand. (Psalm 16:11)*

Often times when we hear the word "joy" we may think of Joy to the
World~ the Christmas carol. Or we conjure up a mental picture of some
oddly-shaped "spiritual fruit" in a cornucopia. For many people the word
"joy" tends to have a "churchy" feel to it. After all, how many people use
the term "joy" in the marketplace or at school? We hear "happy" maybe,
but "joy"?? Not so much.

Most of us don't think of it as a near-tangible substance that has a
physical ability to sustain us! Yet that's what God's Word says about joy~
that it sustains us, that it gives us strength.

As I look around, I see the idea of more strength and happiness as
things we all could use! I see people trying to sustain themselves with

coffee or energy drinks as they run between two jobs to make ends meet in a shaky economy, filling the void with temporary strength. I see them walking around damaged by the world and the cruel things people do to each other. Even the best of us have comments that come out wrong every now and then, which can cause the unintentional wounding of another, creating more holes for both joy and happiness to leak out.

But joy is not just "feel good" happiness~ it goes much deeper than that. God promises that in the midst of a stressful existence He wants to give an internal contentment the world cannot steal! This is just as true today as it was when these words were initially written, despite societal changes. Circumstances today are different: we don't have an evil king waiting at our borders, ready to obliterate us. Nor do we move from cave to cave running for our lives. We have bills, kid issues, employment questions and other challenges. The details of our personal circumstances aren't the issue because God promised that He would be the same yesterday, today and forever! He is the I AM, not the I Was, nor the I Will Be... let that sink in: He is your I AM! The joy He gives is a tangible, valuable gift given every day we ask for it! Joy is found in His presence~ not in the next raise, not in the next shopping trip, or the next new car, or even in the next church activity. We may feel happy as we receive or participate in those things~ but lasting joy comes from seeing Him, spending time with Him, getting direction from Him, being centered in Him!

Dear King of my heart, I seek Your presence, your face~ not just the chance to present You with my to-do list for Your hand of blessing. In Your presence joy comes! You don't deny the pain of life, but You give me strength to overcome it all, and I thank You for that!

In Jesus' Name, Amen

Overcoming Praise

I will bless the Lord at all times; His praise will always be
on my lips...I sought the Lord and He answered me; He
delivered me from all my fears. (Psalm 34:1, 4)

Did you feel like blessing the Lord when you heard that the government bailout deal didn't go through? How about when you got the report that you needed a heart catheter? Or that your dog had to be put down? Or that your child's teacher suddenly died? These aren't the moments when we exactly feel like giving praise, are they? But you know what? God didn't give us an exception to His command here. Why? Because our country's economy isn't our source~ He is! Because He made our heart and knows how it functions, and gave the doctor the wisdom to keep us alive! Because the teacher's family is being comforted, and she knew Christ and was ready to go! Our feelings, as important and as powerful as they are, aren't meant to override the Truth of the matter.

The Truth of the matter is that Jesus Christ is right in the midst of every struggle you have. He sees every tear, He knows the hurt you feel. And He alone has the power to help you overcome! I have friends who have faced two of these above situations recently, one we personally had, and one is impacting the world. I'm soo thankful that my friends know

Christ! We know He is our Source of supply, of comfort, of strength, and the world needs to see the difference in how we face these challenges versus how they face them. Verse four says "I sought the Lord and He answered me. He delivered me from ALL my fears"! Wow, that's powerful, and again, He leaves no exceptions! Why? Because He's an "all inclusive" God! He covers it. If you face it, He's already there with the answer in His hand. True, some things are harder to walk through than others. Some are a piece of cake, while others tug at the very core of our being, threatening to crush us. He is still there. He will deliver you from ALL your fear as you seek Him!

That's the key: we have our part, and He has His part: as we seek Him, the fear disperses, the faith grows, we watch Him move. As we bless the Lord, He begins the process of healing. We don't thank Him because our country is facing a big challenge~ rather we bless Him in the midst of the challenge: that He's here with us, He has the solution to meet our need. He gives us wisdom and strength for our every step.

Father God, I choose to bless Your Holy Name in the midst of my
circumstances today. I receive Your freedom from my fear and the
uncertainty of this world I live in. I thank You for being steady, depend-
able, my all-inclusive provider God! I trust You with my life!

In Jesus' Name, Amen!

Affecting Change

If My people, who are called by My Name, will humble them-selves and pray and seek My face and turn from their wicked ways, then will I hear from heaven and will forgive their sin and will heal their land. (2 Chronicles 7:14)

Many people are familiar with this passage, and it's a very popular one to recite at times like this~ the birthday of our land. Two things to note:

1- it's not directed to non-Christians, but to God's people. People who called Him their God are the ones who needed to get rid of the wickedness, become humble and turn their faces and hearts back to Him. Revival begins in the house of God before it extends to the world. In fact, it is genuine repentance that draws the world to Christ, because they see the result of live, dynamic relationship replacing stale dead religion. Repentance involves turning away from the things that draw our attention away from God and replacing Him on the throne of our lives. Healing follows repentance, not the other way around.

2- It doesn't take the whole country to affect change. We know that "where two or three are gathered in My Name there I am in the midst". Change, revolutionary change, can be sparked by a few faithful people dedicated to a cause. Take a look at the way the eleven disciples flipped the world upside down two thousand years ago with the revelation of Who Jesus is! Look at our own history in the USA~ a seemingly small band of men and women clung tightly to the dream of freedom to worship their God without fear of governmental repercussions and the world superpower of the day fell before them because God was on their side.

We have that opportunity before us again today. Lessons forgotten must be re-learned, and so we stand at the crossroads of our children's future and the existence of our country. Will we check our own lives and stand in the gap for our country before God, or lapse into pop culture ignorance and wake up one day wondering what happened?

God promises He will hear and He will heal. As we do our part, His hand will move on our behalf!

Father God, thank You that I can know Your promises are true, that You back up Your Word with Your power. Lord I repent, ask forgiveness, for sins in my own life. I want to be clean before You. I ask for forgiveness for my nation and the sins she has committed before You. Lord come, heal, restore, as You promised. We are a small group on the landscape of humanity but with You we are an unstoppable majority! May Your Name be praised in all the earth!!

In Jesus' Name, Amen

Lessons from Our Garden

...but the one who received the seed that fell on good soil is the man who hears the Word and understands it. He produces a crop, yielding a hundred, sixty or thirty times what was sown." (Matthew 13:18-23)

"I'm sure I didn't plant any weeds this spring!" I thought as I stood in our garden this past weekend, looking at our mounds of cucumber plants. The veggies were there all right, but almost lost in the weeds.

We had begun starter plants over spring break in peat pots on the table in our sun room, and transplanted them after rototilling and spreading fertilizer in the garden plot. As the veggies had begun to grow, we had made sure to weed through the areas of early harvest, but cucumbers were bearing later than the beans, corn and zucchini, so had received less attention recently.

How parallel is this to our lives? We grow and develop and live our lives. One area calls more loudly for our attention at a specific moment, and other areas of life get less of our attention. Before we know it, voila! There are weeds we didn't plant, and don't want!

As a Christian, having received Jesus as Lord and the filling of the Holy Spirit, we have the best Helper to tend the garden of life we could ever ask for! We still need to oversee the whole garden, but as we put

God first, and listen to the coaching He gives, we know when to tend a specific area of life before the weeds entangle the fruit (or veggies) we want our lives to produce and choke them out. We see the small plants of progress in life grow, knowing the harvest is coming. Our days of watering, weeding, tending, keeping the deer, coons and rabbits out will pay off! Our lives are in the process of becoming like my garden, a thing of beauty and abundant harvest, with much greater return than initial investment! You see, God has an incredible way of causing exponential return on our life-investment when we trust Him with it!

We planted six rows of corn, about fifteen plants each. We have already harvested forty ears, (not counting what the deer and raccoons have munched on) and each ear had many more kernels than I originally planted. Dozens are still on the stalks; now that's exponential return on investment!

Is that the kind of return you'd like to see in your own life: rich and rewarding friendships, a successful marriage full of unconditional love, kids rightly connected with God and having open communication lines with you? Receive Jesus as Lord and allow the Holy Spirit to come in and be your Counselor. Weeding the garden does take a while, but the payoff is eternally worth it!

Dear Heavenly Father, as I look at my life, I see many tangles of weeds.
I don't know where to start, but know I need help to clean it out. Right
now the harvest of my life isn't what I want it to be. Please come in and
be my Lord, forgive my sins and send Your Holy Spirit as my Helper.
I want the eternal, exponential harvest that only You can produce!

In Jesus' Name, Amen

Bushels of Expectation

*All honor to the God and Father of our Lord Jesus Christ, for
it is by his boundless mercy that God has given us the privilege of being born again. Now we live with a wonderful expectation because Jesus Christ rose again from the dead. (I Peter 1:3)*

I was studying our upsy-downsy tomato plant holders; amazed at the
load those pots are carrying this season. So different from last year! The
one who planted had used the coconut mulch that came in the containers but had forgotten to add regular soil or fertilizer. Needless to say, the
results we got out of that batch were negligible from spindly vines and
anemic leaves that couldn't sustain anything healthy.

This year was different! After starting the seedlings inside during
spring break, by Mother's Day they were ready to transplant into the
containers. Because we expected to lose some plants, we started four in
the top and two on the bottom. The results this year have been incredible!
With the addition of proper fertilizer and good soil, we haven't lost a plant!
The harvest has resulted in wonderful fruit from strong plants with thick
vines and big leaves! The challenge this season is to keep them watered
frequently enough to meet the demand of all those plants in each pot and
not lose the plants before they reach their maximum output of potential!

We should have known better. We identified the problem and fixed it, but we should also have changed the expectation, and thus planted differently too.

So much like our Christian walk, isn't it? We realize that without Jesus the "vines" of our relationships and self image more closely resemble those of the first plants- seriously lacking. We meet Him and everything changes! The "vines" begin to grow strong and healthy. The potential harvest of our life has the expectation of new vitality!

But inside sometimes we forget the spiritual changes and "plant" things in our lives based on our former self-image and low expectations. We can miss the correlation between the eternal and the earthly, and slip into the old pattern of expecting nothing more from our efforts that the results we were so used to getting.

As we dig into His Word, our own "instruction manual" on how to be firmly and securely planted in Him, grafted into the Ultimate Vine, the expectation changes. Our minds begin to be transformed into His likeness and reach toward our original design. We quit planting weeds in our own soil. We become secure and quit "over-planting" our pots. We raise our understanding of what it looks like to be fertilized with Spiritual Miracle Grow! The Master Gardener has come to care for us, transplanted us into the fertile soil of the abundant life He planned for us from the beginning!

Father God, my Master Gardener, thank You for the hope You bring to my life, for the spiritual Miracle Grow of Your Word- reliable, trustworthy, unfailing. Please help me to see myself and my circumstances in the light of Your plans and expectations.

In Jesus' Name, Amen

The Hairs on Your Head!

"But the very hairs of your head are numbered. Do
not fear therefore." (Matthew 10:30-31)

Overheard during devotion time: "Wow, God numbered the hairs on my head? Thank You Jesus that I still have some! HAHA!"

At this point in life, a good sense of humor is helpful on many things, but seriously, think about that: if the hairs on my head were important enough to God for Him to number them, how important is all the rest of me to Him? How important are your hairs.,. and the rest of you to Him??

God wants you to understand that you are important. When you accepted Jesus Christ as your Savior you became worthy!! You are worthy of His grace, His love, His passion, His abundance, and His protection from all the enemy's snares... hidden and otherwise.

He just wants a relationship with you! He wants you to spend time with Him in His presence. How cool is that? The Almighty God wants me??? He wants YOU! We should be shouting that from the rooftops! God wants to spend time with all of us, one-on-one individual time with each and every one of us, each and every day! Wow isn't that awesome!

How do we get that time? Start by taking time to pray. Prayer opens that door to heaven and allows the communication to begin. Open your ears and, as the Bible says, "listen for that still small voice." He has your "hair count", He is here and He is ready to meet...are you?

> *Father God, You love us so much You change our "hair count"*
> *each day! We long to be close to You. We ask You to lead and*
> *guide us down the paths that You have designed for us. You*
> *have said that we are worthy of Your love and we choose to*
> *accept that today. We give You the glory and the praise.*
>
> *In Jesus Name, Amen.*

Flocks, Herds and Crowns~ Leadership

Be sure to know the condition of your flocks, give careful atten-
tion to your herds; for riches do not endure forever, and a
crown is not secure for all generations. (Proverbs 28:23-27)

Hmmm...so how are your flocks and herds doing this week? The answer is rhetorical in most cases, since most of us don't have literal flocks and herds these days. How secure is your crown? Again, as similar answer~ we don't wear crowns! So how does this passage apply to us today?

Let's update the lingo without altering the meaning: do you have children? Do you have people in a church small group you lead? Are you an overseer or manager in the workplace? Do you serve or volunteer in any capacity? Those who are under you, for whom you are responsible, who depend on you for a part of their well-being, are your "flocks and herds" these days. Your "crown" is representative of your authority or leadership in whichever capacity you find yourself. Do you lead by title only, or do you personally invest in those whom you lead? Does your team know you care about them, or do they believe you're only looking out for Number One? Will you give up something you have or are entitled to in order to make sure they have what they need, or do you leave them in a place of struggle and wanting, still looking for a leader who will properly care for them? That's a measure of how secure your "crown" is.

So now let's ask again: how are your "flocks and herds"? Is your "crown" or position of authority secure? As you lead in your differing capacities, do you have your priorities lined up? For example in my home, my children are my primary "flocks and herds" followed closely by those who participate in both ministry and business. There are times a pressing need arises, and I adjust my time to allocate it to tend to a business team-mate's need, and put my kids "on hold". There are times it's vice-versa also. The balance is constantly in a state of flux and adjustment~ not at all a static fixture in my life. I've become more conscientious to talk through the changes with my girls so they know what to expect, and don't feel neglected on a particularly busy day. I then make sure to carve out that time with them once again, so we stay on track and connected as we walk through this life as a family. Were I to leave my girls in a state of neglected communication and time, the state of my "flock" wouldn't be very healthy.

There are also times when I have had to make family, business or ministry decisions that are tough, but based on the information I have, and my peace from God, I know they are right. It can throw flocks and herds into temporary questioning, and there again lies the important phrase 'open lines of communication'. If all the decisions we faced were easy, we could sail through life without Holy Spirit guidance and God's strength.

Ultimately, the flocks and herds we each lead must know we have their best interest at heart and be willing to trust our decisions and follow our directions (especially our kids~ that's a whole separate category of leading!). The state of our flocks and herds must be healthy in order to secure our crown. Always remember: as much as we lead others here, we also follow the Best Shepherd, Who will one day judge not only our actions, but the state of our flocks and herds as well. To whom much is given, much is required!

> *Dear Father, thank You for being the best Shepherd ever! I want to follow You, and make You proud of the choices I make. When You return, I want You to be pleased with the state of the "flocks and herds" that You entrusted me with. I want my crown from You to be secure because it's established in righteousness, integrity, justice and above all: love. Give me a true heart for those who trust me to lead or provide for them in some way, so You may be truly glorified in my life!*
>
> *In Jesus' Name, Amen*

Speak It!

*...so is My Word that goes out from My mouth: It will not return
to Me empty but will accomplish what I desire. (Isaiah 55:11)*

*Out of the same mouth come praise and cursing. My broth-
ers this should not be. Can both fresh water and salt
water flow from the same spring? (James 3:10-11)*

*Like a fluttering sparrow or a darting swallow an unde-
served curse does not come to rest. (Proverbs 26:2)*

We know words are seed. You've probably heard it before and I've
written about it before, however I need to go there again. We have an
important role in creating the life we live. Yes God is the Author of life,
and while I won't pretend to usurp His position, we do need to realize
that we were never intended to live like dead fish floating downstream,
whisked along by the current, willingly accepting everything that comes
along! God wants us to take an active role in our own lives and partner
with Him! God create the world in the first place by speaking it into being!
Since we are not Him, we can't quite go there, but we can creatively impact

our personal world, and the sphere of influence and dominion He has given us here with our own words, following His example.

He watches over His Word to perform it. So the flip side is: if we aren't saying His Word, He won't perform it~ not because He is unwilling, but because it hasn't been commissioned into our lives. Think of a situation you want Him to work in to cause a specific outcome in your life... What Scripture are you standing on, quoting and praying over that situation to have the greatest God-impact possible on it? Have you listened to your mouth, do you really want Him to do what He hears you saying?

An undeserved curse will not come to rest. Are you speaking blessing or curses on people and situations around you? If what someone is saying about you isn't true, you don't have to worry, because as you give it to God He will keep it from coming to rest upon you. Now, let's flip it again: are the things you are saying about other people true? If not it will come back on you. Do your words honor God? Do they build up the Body? If what you're saying isn't true, you need to line it up with Truth. If not, the wages you'll pay on your words will be heavier than you really care to stumble under.

God says both blessings and curses shouldn't come out of the same mouth. He gives the example that you never see a spring with both salt water and fresh water~ it's one or the other, never both.

Here's a silly but real example I saw recently: a woman speaker was given a gift bag in her hotel room upon arrival at the event, and the bag contained some chocolate. She was trying to lose weight but felt very tempted with the sweet treat. When she began her talk, she announced that "whoever gave me that chocolate~ I hate you!" She laughed, and repeated it about three more times, thinking she was funny. She then proceeded to talk about God's love. It felt like both salt water and fresh water flowing from the same spring. Both the attempt at humor and the message of the moment were lost due to her incompatible words. In the same way she needed to watch her words so her message wasn't lost, so must we watch our words. They are the seed for our future!

Dear Heavenly Father, keep my words pure, like fresh cool water, so others may neither be hurt by them nor confused as to my intent, especially when it comes to my testimony for You. I choose to honor You and speak Your life into my daily situations, creating Your best in my sphere!

In Jesus' Name, Amen

A Time to Mourn

There is a time for everything, and a season for every activ-
ity under heaven: a time to be born and a time to die, a time to
plant and a time to uproot, a time to weep and a time to laugh, a
time to mourn and a time to dance... (Ecclesiastes 3: 1, 2, 4)

That's the verse that came to mind today as I sat out on my deck reading my Bible. The skies were gray and the air thick with humidity, tempting the rain to fall. Just then a break in the clouds illuminated a rainbow- not the full arc, just what some would call a "sundog"~ a small but brilliant piece of the whole thing.

There has been some rain in my life this week, too~ joys, but also significant rain. Just as there is a time to rejoice in the blessings of life, there is also an appropriate time to grieve a loss. I encourage you: let your grieving be pure!

Grief is a part of healthy human emotion, but just as anything else taken to the extreme is not healthy, neither is grieving. There is actually a spirit of grief (different than the emotion of grief) that can come in to tangle us in that vulnerable place if we stay too long. God knew this too, which is why for His people He set aside specific time to grieve and experience the full gamut of the emotion, but then He also limited the time of staying in that place of mourning.

What removes that spirit? Praise! Joy! There is a time for sadness and mourning which is always to be followed by a time of praise and joy. Weeping may last for a night, but joy comes in the morning! It's a spiritual principle.

Some folks may try to prevent you from having the time to mourn a loss, calling you "weak" and telling you to "get your emotions under control" while others won't want you to move out of mourning and into joy. Be aware; stay tuned into the Holy Spirit, because neither extreme is healthy. God gave us these emotions when He made us in His image, in full knowledge of what He was giving us. When we give them back to Him, He helps us process them all. Just as I only saw a piece of the rainbow, I don't as yet see all that He's working on behind the scenes. He sees the complete picture, while I see and understand only in part, but that part is growing, and I trust Him to help me process the sorrows of life hand in hand with Him.

Father God, please take my jumble of emotions. You know best how to sort them out, and how I can feel them without letting them rule me. Teach me to experience them and keep them healthy. I give them back to You. Please carry me through and keep me in balanced step with You, as a complete being: spiritual, physical and emotional. Thank You for the gift of being able to feel all aspects of this life You give on earth!

In Jesus' Name, Amen

Faithfulness

*But My faithfulness and My mercy will be with him. And in
My Name his strength will be exalted. (Psalm 89: 24)*

We have an amazing puppy! Okay, so she qualifies as a dog now~ she
just turned two today! She is a beautiful black lab-golden retriever mix,
with a soft and shiny black coat and big brown eyes. Freedom is a great
example of love and faithfulness in our family. For example, when the
kids are playing at the beach or swimming she stays right with them~ no
lie: you can watch her do a "head count" to make sure everyone is present
and accounted for. She won't come up to the house from the beach until
the last child has left the water and is on her way up!

One of my favorite water stories with her comes from last summer,
when she was just a pup. One of the younger girls was in the shallows of
the lake, maybe knee-deep, goofing around with the rest, and fell face-first
into the water. Because it wasn't deep, the child wasn't scared or hurt, but
boy was she surprised when Freedom grabbed the back of her swimsuit
and pulled her up out of the water!!

One other story from this summer: a younger child and his family
made a first visit to our home; he was brave in the lake in his water ring,
and swam out quite a distance past the dock. When Freedom felt he had

gone far enough, she swam out near him, hit his floatie with her nose and swam back toward the dock. He didn't follow. She repeated. He didn't follow. After he didn't follow her for the third time, she began to swim circles around him, preventing him from going out any farther. It was amazing to watch! She is a faithful dog.

God is faithful to us in such ways that makes these stories pale in comparison. He, too, watches over us. He is unwilling any should die in sin. He has spared us all from some consequences, pulling us up "by our britches". He nudges us not with His nose, as Freedom did, but with the Holy Spirit, using the unrest in our hearts or external circumstances to help us identify when we're straying from the proper course or out of safe waters. He designed each of us with a specific destiny in His mind and equipped us with the dreams in our hearts to be able to accomplish them. He is so faithful that He created a Life Raft for us to grab on to as we swim through this existence~ and His Name is Jesus Christ!

Have you grabbed onto Him by asking Him into your heart? Do you pay attention to His warnings about how far out to swim? Do you follow His lead to swim back toward shore, trusting that He knows what's ahead, knowing that in His eternal faithfulness, He will direct you not just toward the good, but ultimately toward the Best this life, and the next, have to offer??

Dear Father, thank You for Your faithfulness to nudge me back into the right and safe direction, toward Your Best! I choose to receive Your faithful re-directs as guidance and protection instead of getting annoyed at Your changes from my own plan. Thank You for showing faithfulness to the point of sacrificing Jesus to reach me, yes even me!

In Jesus' Name, Amen

The Depth of Love

For God so loved the world that He gave His only begotten Son, that who-soever believes in Him should not die but have eternal life. (John 3:16)

And I pray that you, being rooted and established in love, may have power together with all the saints, to grasp how wide and long and high and deep is the love of Christ, and to know this love that surpasses knowledge~ that you may be filled to the measure of all the fullness of God. (Ephesians 3:17b-19)

Today is a big day for celebration in our house: we added a new puppy to our household! It was not a spur-of-the-moment thing. We researched online, looking at the different breeds, temperaments, ages and asking price. The girls plowed through websites for puppy rescues and identified our preferred breeds as far away as Missouri (!) which we said were out of range. We did the work to narrow our preferences, and today made the journey to a store hosting a pet adoption day, paid the fee... and came home with a new little girl!

The prep-work we did for this new addition is nothing compared to the work God did when He chose you! In fact, He did more than choose you, He made you! He didn't simply speak you into existence, but bent down over the dust of the earth, gently carving your cheeks, selecting your hair and eye color, your basic temperament and giftings- just right to complete the assignment He designed specifically for you. God took time and care. He fashioned you unique from every other creation He has ever made, yet made you in His image. You are His most precious of all, His beloved!

Now let's add the next dimension: sin entered the picture and you were separated from God (we all were). His heart never stopped loving you! His loving Father-arms ached to hold you again. He knew you were in the clutches of His arch-enemy who would abuse and mistreat you. When He sought you out, you were in the enemy's kennel: bruised, hungry, lonely, in need of rescue, ready to be sold to the highest bidder for the next go-round; He stepped in and paid the full asking price. No negotiations. No questions in His heart. No research needed. No re-evaluation of the situation. He never thought "I wonder if this person is still worth it after all the damage s/he has been through?" He just paid the price. What was required was one drop of perfect blood. Jesus wanted no doubt in your mind about how much He loved you, or the validity of the fee He paid~ so He gave it all; every last drop of blood. His life for yours. End of discussion, no more questions about His desire to buy you back and meet your every need. Unquenchable love.

Father God, thank You that Your love for me is so unfathomably more than I could ever ask or imagine! Thank You for removing all doubt about my value in your eyes. Thank You for my rescue!

In Jesus' Name, Amen

Major League Soldier

Jesus said "It is written..." (Matthew 4:4, 7,10)

*and out of His mouth came a sharp dou-
ble-edged sword (Revelation 1:16b)*

*But what does it say? The word is near you; it is in your
mouth and in your heart. (Romans 10:8a)*

*The weapons we fight with are not the weapons of
this world. On the contrary, they have divine power
to demolish strongholds. (2 Corinthians 10:4)*

*They defeated (the Antichrist) by the Blood of the Lamb &
by the word of their testimony. (Revelation 12:11a)*

Is spiritual warfare real, or is it just something we read about when we pick up books by authors like Ted Dekker or Frank Peretti? Do we really fight technicolor demons? If so, how do we defeat the enemy we face?

Ephesians 6 lists the weapons God has given us, and the author likens them to the pieces worn by Roman soldiers, so that what he wrote was very contemporary to the generation to whom he was speaking. Of all the pieces listed, which include breastplate/ helmet/ shield/ sandals/ belt, the only offensive piece is the sword, specifically the Sword of the Spirit, which is the Word of God.

Today we may see these pieces in a museum or on display in a private collection, but we don't see them physically used in combat like they did then. Unfortunately, that's the way many Christians behave with this weapon as well~ but that's not what God intended!

We may not see technicolor demons flying around, needing to be sliced out of the sky, but we do face illnesses like cancer and flu, don't we? Or how about relational challenges that lead to divorce even in "good Christian homes"? Behind each of these situations is a demon that went unchallenged, the Sword was not employed as it should have been. How do we activate it? God says in the Old Testament that He is watching over His Word to perform it. He says in the New Testament that we will overcome (the enemy) by the Blood of the Lamb and the word of our testimony. God did His part~ He sent Jesus to shed His perfect blood so we could be reunited with God the Father. After we choose to receive this price paid, we do our part by speaking out our testimony to others of how He has and is working in our lives. Not only that but we are to speak out the Word of God itself! To read the Bible silently is almost the equivalent of taking the sleek, ornate, finely balanced sword out of its glass case and run our fingers over the broad side as we admire it. To speak out His Word is to use it and activate it in battle, defeating the germs that attack our bodies, putting to flight the gnats of demons that buzz around our relationships and cutting down the unseen enemy.

God intended for this Sword to be hung by our side, ready to do battle at a moments' notice, on alert to speak out His Word that has been hidden in our hearts for just such an occasion as this. We are the Lord's anointed, and as such, we are His ambassadors to this lost world. He expects us to operate in His authority to cut the power of the enemy in our life and that of our family. Think about it: how many laid back, casual soldiers do you see in the midst of battle in today's combat movies? What did Jesus do? He used the Sword of God's Word in His confrontation with the devil~ do we think we can do better than He? I think we would do well to follow His example!

If it's easier for you, picture yourself instead as a player on a Major League Baseball team, stepping up to the plate, making solid hit after solid hit, the consistent player your team can count on. If you've ever played, you know the feel of a solid hit the moment contact is made~ how your hands vibrate, the depth of the sound, and you just know the ball is on its way to the outfield.

The same is true here: make a solid hit with the Word of God~ He promises it will hit its mark every time because He will guide it. Just as a soldier doesn't generally make only one swing to take out his opponent, neither will the baseball player take only one swing and be finished. Baseball has nine innings~ not just one "out". Battle has no timeframe~ it goes until one side quits or is eliminated.

Here's a real-life example: our friend's son had been hit by the H1N1 flu. He had all the symptoms for forty-eight hours when his mom began quoting Psalm 91 over him not once, but every hour. His fever of 103+ was broken within six hours and all symptoms vanished~ she won, she battled out loud with the Sword of the Spirit until the enemy left. What a testimony she and her family have now!

To "observe" the Word isn't enough. To "nicely review" the Word won't get the job done~ that's no more than admiring the Word as a shiny, sculpted souvenir. Get it out and battle with it, speaking His Word in authority. Get feisty! It's ok to get loud about it~ I give you permission! If you don't fight, the enemy wins and you miss your destiny. Which do you prefer?

Father God, In the Name of Jesus I partner with You and take hold of the wisdom to do battle in a manner pleasing to You, in accordance with Your will, as You intended it to be done, that I may win victories in my own life, in my family and help those I love to do the same. I don't want Your Word to be a relic in a showcase, but an active tool in my life, that I may please You and fulfill the destiny You created me for!

In Jesus' Name, Amen!

Free from the Leash of Limitations

Therefore, I urge you, brothers, in view of God's mercy, to offer your bodies as living sacrifices, holy and pleasing to God- this is your spiritual act of worship. Do not conform any longer to the pattern of this world, but be transformed by the renewing of your mind. Then you will be able to test and approve what God's will is -His good, pleasing and perfect will. (Romans 12:1-2)

My puppy-girl Freedom goes everywhere with me, since she loves to travel in the car as well as go for walks. The other day after we got home from a ride, I noticed she still had her leash on her, and figured I'd get to it as soon as I finished taking care of my arm load of things. After a few moments she began whining at me, standing in the doorway to our bedroom. I told her "come here", but she didn't move. I figured she just wanted outside again, so re-focused on what I was doing. She whined again, and again I looked up, calling her to me. She didn't come, so the third time she whined I asked her "What do you need, pup?" This time I noticed her leash was caught under the door to our room. It wasn't that she didn't want to come to me but that she couldn't. I walked right over and freed her leash from under the door. Again I went back to what I was doing, and a fourth time she whined to me. She still thought she was stuck, even though she had been set free! I walked over her, reassured her, took gentle hold of her collar and walked her into the kitchen where I had been working. Her expression changed from tense to relaxed as she realized she was no longer stuck, but again free to move around the house with no limitations.

How often do we do that? We have sinned, we feel guilty. We feel we can't get back to God on our own. There's an obstacle, a separation between us that we are powerless to overcome. Jesus came in, paid the price and set us free from "our leash being stuck under the door". He paid the price for our sin, closing the gap between us and God.

Yet sometimes we still stand, unmoving, in the same place, seeing what we want to attain but not believing we are able to~ not good enough, not worthy of, or couldn't ever reach that place.

If we ask Him for help, allow His Word to penetrate our hearts and give us revelation while He transforms our minds, He will smile at us, "take us by the collar" and walk us to our intended destination.

The Truth sets us free! He who has the Son has life and now we are free indeed! Those old mental "tapes" that play in our minds of our former limitations need to be thrown off, cast down! They don't define us anymore! We need to renew our minds to the Truth of God's Word! We don't walk in them anymore~ we are new creations! We are empowered, not because we are "so good" or "so special" or "so worthy" in and of ourselves, but because we are bought with the precious blood of Jesus! He exchanged our "stuck leash" of limitations for His own righteousness and the "freedom to move around the house"! How liberating is that??

How do you see yourself? Are you willing to step into the new season God is leading you into, trusting the mobility He has given you or do you stop short of the destiny He said you can fulfill, thinking your leash is still stuck? Trust Him when He says you are free!

Father God, I love You, and I choose now to allow You to renew my mind and to believe I can do what You said I can do, that I am who You say I am, and that together we can accomplish what You say I can.

In Jesus' Name, Amen!

Do You Deserve a Break Today?

*The harvest is plentiful, but the workers are few. Ask
the Lord of the harvest, therefore, to send out workers into His harvest field. (Matthew 9:37-38)*

*Always be prepared to give an answer to everyone who
asks you to give the reason for the hope that you have. But
do this with gentleness and respect. (I Peter 3:15b)*

Labor Day~ a day to celebrate from our labor and take a well-
deserved break from all we do, week in and week out. A reward for all
the overtime we've put in and problems we've solved in our professional
or working lives. It's a day to take off and come back from it refreshed
and ready to go! Here in Michigan it's the last big "hurrah" for camping
and boating before kids return to school tomorrow.

How is our spiritual gauge for needing a break from our labor? Have
we done enough to deserve a break? Jesus said that the harvest was great,
but the workers were few, and gave the command for us to go hit the
field of souls and lovingly gather them in. Have we? How many people
have you shared your faith with recently? How many have come to know
more about Who Jesus is through your example and mine? Never mind

the concept of "overtime" ~ have we put in much of any time, thought or focus into His harvest?

I spoke with a woman not long ago who met someone new at church. At the end of the service, the new gal was obviously moved and hurting emotionally. All my friend knew to say was "have a great week!" which she knew really didn't fit the circumstance. The moment to reach into the harvest field came and she was unprepared. Though she had sat in church that day, she didn't have The Word in her to give out.

I've been there~ an unexpected moment, caught off guard, not knowing exactly what or how much to say. Peter told us to have a ready answer for whoever asks. Since my personal moment like that, I've made it a point to dig in to the Word so it wouldn't ever happen again. The bottom line is this: we cannot give what we do not have. If we don't have God's Word in us, we can't give it to others, or point them to Him with any manner of effectiveness! God's Word is life. It is health. It is truth. It is salvation. We, as His representatives, must get His Word into us so we can turn around and give it out to others who soooo desperately need it, need Him! If we, who call ourselves by Christ's Name, are not able to point the lost and hurting of this world to Him, where do we expect them to turn? The Church is not a building~ no, the Church is His Body, you and me, His hands and feet!

We must get His Words into our hearts so it can come out our mouths and impact our world! He, through "we", is the Light of the world, so let's go shine!!

Dear Father, I want to be full of Your Word so You can touch this world through me! You have created me with a sense of destiny inside that I need to explore, and which can only be fulfilled by walking through this life hand in hand with You. Show me today what passage You would have me read and think on, so it is fresh in my heart when You call on me to give it to one in need.

In Jesus' Name, Amen

Run for the Prize!

Do you not know that in a race all the runners run, but only one get the prize? Run in such a way as to get the prize. (I Corinthians 9:24)

Inspiration can come from many sources. Recently in my life, my eleven-year-old daughter has been an inspiration to me. She entered middle school, and tried out for cross country. The very next day was her first meet, and she "medaled", running a 7.22 minute mile, beating every girl from her grade, and all but three boys from all other participating schools! Since then, she has run two other races, and put up times that now allow her to train with the fastest girl in the school. Talk about inspiration!

I had been a runner in middle school also, but ended up tearing ligaments in my ankle. After healing from that, I ended up with shin splints and RSD, which landed me in a walking cast for three months. After that, I quit trying, figuring the pain of recovery wasn't worth the enjoyment I got out of the competition. I maintained my competitive view on life, wanting to do everything I do with excellence, but choosing foosball instead of running. As a Mom of three girls now, I had relegated myself to the role of "softball Mom", "piano Mom", "room Mom" or "ice skating Mom", but not "5k running Mom"! Watching my daughter these last few weeks, though, has re-opened my personal love of the sport, and tapped a piece of me I had put away for a long time.

Running a race is the analogy the Apostle Paul uses for living the Christian life. Instead of running a predictable life on a straight smooth track, life in this world is much more similar to the world of cross country running: over the hills, splashing through the puddles, and around the grassy fields. All of us are here on our own course, planted deep inside us by our Master Creator! There are times when we run with others; there are times when our only Companion is our Lord. Some people think they can wander through the fields and pick the wildflowers instead of running the race that is life. Some pretend there is no greater calling or responsibility on them than to play in the mud puddle right in the middle of the course and watch everyone else run past.

But God has "put eternity in our hearts". There's a piece of us that knows we were destined for more! God is a gentleman; He wants us to know His plan, and He wants us to reach for Him to find it instead of forcing it upon us. As a result there come crossroads in our lives that He orchestrates so we have to look to Him instead of ourselves. We lose our way in the field of wildflowers and don't know where to go to head back to the course. It has rained, and washed out parts of the course chalk lines, all the trees we pass look the same... what now?

Did you know the Bible says ALL things are possible through Christ Who loved us? He knows exactly where we are, and how to get us back onto our intended course~ so what if we've taken some detours! He knows the plan, and He knows how to get us where we need to be to fulfill our destiny! This side of heaven it's never too late! All we have to do is ask for help, then trust Him enough to do what He says.

By the way, I'm back on the running trail, and though I'm not expecting to beat my daughter any time soon, I know that I can be more than what I've given myself credit for in this area of life, because all things are possible in Christ!

Dear Father God, Forgive me for time lost in the mud puddles of life! Thank you for receiving my wilting bouquet of wildflowers of my own works with mercy and grace, and for re-directing me back onto my intended course. I want to run my life in step with You, and in such a way as to please You, Daddy! Thank you for restoring me, and never giving up on me. With You, ALL things are possible, and I commit myself to You today.

In Jesus' Name, Amen

Pray for Israel

For Zion's sake I will not remain silent till her righteousness shines out like the dawn, her salvation like a blazing torch. I have posted watchmen on your walls, O Jerusalem; they will never be silent day or night.

You who call on the Lord give yourselves no rest, and give Him no rest till He establishes Jerusalem and makes her the praise of the earth. (Isaiah 62: 1, 6-7)

Hundreds of times in the Bible God calls the city of Jerusalem "His City". Jerusalem is often personified as not just a woman, but as "His Bride". We read how "she seeks Him" or "she turns away from Him into the arms of other lovers" (the figurative language of following other gods) and then comes rushing back to Him after a period of judgment and destruction. He makes it clear all throughout that He loves Jerusalem with an everlasting love. He wrote the end of the story, so we know Jerusalem does indeed become His Bride, exalted above all nations.

We're not to that chapter of the Book yet though, are we? All we have to do is turn on the news to see that we're still in the part of the Book where Jerusalem has been away from God~ but is desperately seeking to come back to Him as evidenced by revival beginning inside the nation.

As a result she is hated throughout the world. Anti- Semitism is now at an all-time high since the Nazi extermination of millions of them in their ovens during the Holocaust. No one but the USA historically has stood politically with Israel and now even that is questionable at best. Something is wrong when illegal aliens are welcomed to drain U.S. economic resources, but folks of Jewish heritage who have lived here peacefully, legally and paid their taxes for decades are threatened with their very lives~ told to "go back to the ovens", as was videotaped in an Arab Muslim demonstration in Fort Lauderdale, Florida recently.

Why? What's happening? The Name of Jesus Christ is a lightening rod, splitting good and evil. His people are not welcome because neither is He in a world where "principalities, powers and rulers of this dark age" are exalted. The closest the enemy can get to striking back at God is to viciously attack Israel and God's people, which include Jews, Messianic Jews and Christians.

There is no doubt that the nation of Israel has her issues~ look at the United States, don't we also? Every country does! But the fact of the matter is that God wrote the Book so we know how the Story ends. Either we trust Him to fulfill His every Word, or we don't. He warned us again and again that those who defend Israel will be blessed with the blessings of Abraham, but those who turn away from her will be cursed. This isn't a political issue; it's a spiritual one.

How does this apply to you and me today? Our Christian heritage is grounded in Judaism. A threat to Jerusalem and the very existence of the nation of Israel is a threat against you and me. History repeats itself unless the lessons learned are remembered by the next generation. It wasn't just Hitler who murdered the Jews, but the whole German society turned against them, even doctors performed horrible experiments on them at will, not just under Nazi threat... and any Christian who tried to help them received the similar treatment.

There's no time left for riding the fence. God ordered all of us who call upon His Name- not just the Jews- to call out for the peace of Jerusalem, until she is exalted and made a jewel among the nations of the world. We need to pray for her, her leaders, her decisions, her proper boundaries to be secure. We can, by our prayers of faith, shorten these days for her and for ourselves also. Pray for our nation to turn back toward her in a favorable way, or the judgment being levied against her enemies will include us, growing worse until it becomes almost unbearable. In The Book, worldwide economic crumbling prepares the way for the anti-Christ and Israel stands alone, isolated from all support but God. Many believe we are watching the set-up of this circumstance. Yet in the midst of a very dark time God will still bless those who call upon His Name and meet our needs on all levels in a way the world cannot understand.

Evil prevails very simply: when good men and women stand by and do...nothing.

My heart cry for us all today is that we pray for the peace of Jerusalem. It's the only way to face this turbulent time in such a way that we come out on the other side blessed and exalted by Father God.

Father God, I lift up my voice in prayer today for the nation of Israel. Lord, turn the hearts of her people, especially her leaders, toward You. May her choices reflect Your wisdom, love and peace. In Your power, protect her borders and her people. Help her to see clearly through the myriad of circumstances swirling around her, choosing in a way that honors You. Grant her protection from the enemies on all sides who seek to destroy her; may all attacks be thwarted. May all who defend her and pray for her be blessed in obedience. May Your Name be exalted throughout the earth!

In Jesus' Name, Amen

God Heals Gently

*Come to me, all you who are weary and burdened, and I will give
you rest. Take My yoke upon you and learn from Me, for I am
gentle and humble in heart, and you will find rest for your souls.
For My yoke is easy and My burden light. (Matthew 11:28-30)*

Have you ever noticed God at work in your life, healing a broken area? I have. He's done it enough for me to recognize a pattern; perhaps it's similar in your life...

In the natural progression of good relationships, they deepen with time and connection. As this developed in one specific couple- friendship I have, I began to get uncomfortable. Unwittingly, one person of the couple had hit a tender spot in my soul~ a wound caused by someone else, and I began to pull back. A friend recognized what was happening and we discussed it a couple times, but my emotional guard had gone up as a matter of self-protection.

I began to think about and pray about what to do. I did not want to let go of my protective posture. I had no interest in experiencing more of the same in that area of life! As I contemplated the situation and my options, God began to speak to me not so much in prayer but more in fleeting thoughts and realizations across my mind. They were brief at first, then grew more clear, and more direct. He was gently bringing me to a point where my own reading of His Word, the Bible- based messages at church, and His powerful presence and personal work in me during worship was penetrating my walls. Finally I melted into His safe and loving arms, and a pile of tears. I saw the initial hurt, generated years ago and hiding under layers. I spoke God's healing over it and chose to forgive the person really responsible. In the process I released the person in our new friendship from his part of things, and in so doing saw a larger part of God's plan. This person hadn't been sent to annoy or further wound me but to cause a holy discomfort leading to a greater degree of awareness followed by healing!

God then showed me my similarity to a cracked glass. I want to be whole, to contain more and more of Him, yet when there's a crack in the side of my glass, His presence and power leak out. As I let Him heal it, soldering me back together, not only can I hold more of Him as a useful container but I reflect His beauty in a myriad of prismatic color!

Perhaps you have an area of life that "cracked your glass"~ or even splintered it into a million pieces that look impossible to reassemble. Well, you're right: on your own they are just that. But that's where He enters the scene. He was there when the initial damage was done to you, like He was with me too, even if we didn't recognize His presence and desire to protect us. Today we see Him here alongside us. He has healing in His hands for you, too. As you, like I, allow Him to go to work on those cracks and splinters, an amazingly intricate and beautiful design begins to emerge. He heals gently, drawing you to Himself~ your Safe Place, taking you one step at a time, as you are ready to release the damage to Him in exchange for the gentle healing power in His hands.

Father God my Healer, You Know I have broken places from this worlds' imperfections just like everyone else. Your grace, mercy and power are beautiful things at these moments of life, and I receive Your gentle healing.... Thank You for Your restoration in me.

In Jesus' Name, Amen

The Peaceful Guide

*For as many as are led by the Spirit of God, they
are the sons of God. (Romans 8:14)*

When you need God's input on something, what do you do? How do you ask when you need His wisdom? How we ask can impact the answers we see.

I used to follow Gideon's example. He is a guy from the Old Testament (first section of the Bible) whom God instructed through a personal visit from an angel to lead the people of Israel as a Judge. He wasn't sure about all this: it was a huge step for him to take since he was waaaayyyy down "on the totem pole" as far as societal influence was concerned. He inquired of God to be sure of his calling and placed a "fleece" (piece of wool) before God. One day, at his prayer request, it was wet with dew but the ground around it was dry; the next day it was the opposite~ again in response to his request. He took his sign from God and stepped in to the opportunity to lead the people as he had been appointed to do.

I had been taught that this was one way to receive an answer from God. Since we don't live in an agricultural society anymore, the phrase "lay out a fleece before God" has grown to become a symbolic term for the prayer 'God, give me this particular sign to answer me with 'yes' and that particular sign for 'no'".

While it's true God can still lead us in that manner, today we actually have a better and more secure way to follow God and be sure we know His will!

The above verse has changed how I pray, and how I look for God. While it's always fun to see pieces falling into place, I don't rely on the limitations of circumstances around me to get the guidance and wisdom I need from my Heavenly Daddy. He has given all of us who believe in Him the internal presence and witness of Holy Spirit as our guide! As Romans puts it, we who are the sons of God are led by the Spirit of God! Have you heard the phrase "go with your peace" when it comes to making a decision? Well, here's the Bible backing to support that comment.

Hint: your peace will ALWAYS line up with Biblical principle, (which is a whole extended topic and not the focus of this devo...)

Holy Spirit really does give an internal heart-peace that the world can't understand, and it has nothing to do with making sense in your own head! Some people call it "a gut feeling" or "an unction". Have you ever had the experience of usually going home a certain route, but that day you just couldn't, and for some reason you took a different road, only to hear later about the fatal accident at that intersection~ at the exact time you would have been there? Or maybe it was a job transition: things looked fine and you were happy where you were, but then this nagging feeling inside told you to submit your resume with a different company. You took the new job and six months later your previous employer was out of business? Those are simple examples of how the Holy Spirit can lead us. It doesn't matter if others understand, or if we can logically explain it~ we just know there's a certain thing we need to do~ or not do. Once we comply, we're filled with a sense of peace that we've made the right choice. The better we listen, and the more readily we respond in trust, the better we hear His voice, until we have almost a "zero hesitation factor" to follow Him immediately.

The enemy still has the ability to test us by messing with circumstances around us, but no one and nothing can take away the peace that Holy Spirit gives!

Father God, thank You for the awesome gift You gave me in the Holy Spirit! Today I will consult You with my decisions, listen for Your voice, and look for Your peace in the midst of my circumstances.

In Jesus' Name, Amen

Eternity in our Hearts

He has put eternity in our hearts. (Ecclesiastes 3:11b)

You will seek Me and find Me when you seek Me with your whole heart. I will be found by you. (Jeremiah 29:13-14)

God did this so that men would seek Him and perhaps reach out for Him and find Him, though He is not far from us. (Acts 17:22-28, v.27)

Sunday afternoon was beautiful, though cold. I worked out on the deck to clean off the patio table for the season, and my puppy ran through the yard in complete glee at her restored freedom from the house. The last several days had been very rainy and blustery, so she had been resigned to watch wistfully out the window as the squirrels and chipmunks scampered, unable to initiate the chase. Today, however, was a different story as she intently gave pursuit. She even splashed through the lake, and then jumped around the beach. Finally she set into digging wholeheartedly, flinging sand to the far side of our beach, all the while a big smile clearly visible on her face.

I didn't have to teach her to dig~ God gave her instincts for life as a dog. (I did get to teach her that the only place she's allowed to dig is the beach!) She instinctively knows how to do all the things she needs to live. With my girls, however, it is totally different! The only instincts people have are fear of the dark, fear of loud noises and fear of falling. Everything else, I need to teach them.

Actually the Bible tells of us a third thing inherent in each of us that we could refer to as an instinct. God says He has set eternity in our hearts. In other words each of us has a God-shaped void inside that we all fill~ if not with Him, His love, His power and sense of destiny, then with counterfeits: people, things, substances, money, success, power, a fetish, an addiction, legalism, anything we can come up with. The void will be filled, one way or another. We instinctively know there's more to this life than what we see around us. Every culture has developed religious beliefs, someone to worship, something to attribute their lives to, some power greater than themselves that they give credit to.

Try as we might, none of these man-made gods or other idols we place in the spot reserved for the One True God will fit, fill it, or satisfy the hunger deep in our hearts~ and that's intentional, by design. All creation points us to Him~ the Creator and Fulfiller of our need. It's instinctive to look for Him, and He promises that as we look for Him, we will find Him. It's a written guarantee!

Father God, You have set eternity in my heart, and I know there's more to this life than the piece I see. You are here, You made me, and I choose to fill my heart with the reality of Who You are!

In Jesus' Name, Amen

Eye of God

By day the Lord went ahead of them in a pillar of cloud to guide them on their way and by night in a pillar of fire to give them light, so that they could travel by day or night. Neither the pillar of cloud by day nor the pillar of fire by night left its place in front of the people. (Exodus 13:21-22)

I will instruct you and teach you in the way you should go: I will counsel you and guide you with My eye. (Psalm 32:8)

This morning while I was out with my puppy for our morning exercise, I was struck by the fall beauty. Chickadees chirped in the trees, squirrels scampered from tree to tree with mouths full of nuts, and the ground smelled of the fresh saturation from the gentle overnight mist. All at once Heaven pierced the clouds on my left with the Eye of God, as it were, flooding through the crack in the dark rain clouds to reveal brilliant sunshine! It spread across the road in front of me and to my right, illuminating the woods beyond the field, setting ablaze the tree leaves with striking yellows and ambers~ a vivid contrast to more dark rain clouds that back-dropped them. It was breathtaking! After a short bit of time, the sun continued to rise, and passed beyond that specific opening in the clouds. The sharpness of the colors relaxed, no longer the focus of such intense light.

How that is like our walk with God! There are times when we see His hand moving directly upon us, and our lives are ablaze with His discernment and direct interaction! Then His position shifts because His desire is to take us higher and higher in Him, like the sun moving higher into the sky, up and beyond the crack in the cloud directly above us. Though He is still there, the intensity of our interaction relaxes and the colors around us dim, no longer ablaze.

When He moves, we first of all must notice and be aware. Secondly we must make a choice: are we comfortable outside the intensity of vivid interaction we once shared, or will we walk forward with Him as the children of Israel did in the wilderness, again finding ourselves under the direct light of the Eye of God?

If we decide to move forward there will be change ~ whether it is how we worship and walk with Him, the church we attend, the friends we hang out with, the job we have, or anything else you care to list. He is moving forward. Will we let go of our status quo?

What does He expect from us as He moves? I can't answer what He may be putting His finger on for you; I can only answer it for me. Are we chasing God, spending time with Him in praise, worship and seeking His face in prayer and Bible study? Remember: revelation on how to move with Him comes in worship.

In a book called God Chasers, by Tommy Tenney, he describes how fresh revelation from God is what the Table of Shewbread represented in the Tabernacle: hot, fresh from the oven, delicate odor wafting through the air, calling "Come! Take a bite." It's like the brilliance that lit up my walk under the Eye of God, that direct and intense interaction, consistently moving up into the "new".

Many people are in a place of contentment, settling for yesteryear's move of God. The bread of revelation is no longer hot and fresh~ only stale crumbs remain. No more vivid light on their path. It was a good season while it lasted, but they were too comfortable to move out, follow God and get the next fresh loaf~ similar to being in the shadows after the Eye of God passed me by on my walk. Or in the place the Israelites would have been had they refused to follow the pillars of smoke and fire that guided them through the wilderness into their prepared place of promise.

Will we remain content where we are, or seek after Him with all of our hearts, chasing to stay in the Eye of God, desiring connection with Him as we desire the melt-in-our-mouth, fresh, hot bread, just taken from the oven?

O God, may my desire be for You and Your fresh revelation! May I desire to walk in Your light above everything else! May I be willing to move forward, step in step with You, regardless!

In Jesus' Name, Amen

Motivation to Overcome

You were running a good race, who cut in on you to
keep you from obeying the truth? (Galatians 5:7)

My oldest daughter runs cross country. I get lots of great lessons from God during the experiences I watch her grow through, and today I want to share one more with you.

There was one meet I missed, and in hindsight it's probably a good thing. She wears one ankle band since straining it early in the season. This particular meet happened to be hosted at a school with whom she had competed before. She knew one girl in particular would be her main competition: she had lost to the girl once, but had beaten her twice.

Just after the gun shot starting the race, one of the teammates of this girl kicked my daughter right in her tender ankle, completely knocking her down and taking her out of the quick lead she is known to take. She had a choice at that split-second: she had been "cut off"; would she stay down and lose the race, focusing on the injustice and the pain she was in, or get up, get after it and do her best anyway?

How often do we find ourselves in that position? How often do we anticipate those around us to respond positively to our choice of change and growing closer to God, only to be met with the disappointment of name-calling, intimidation, or even scoffing and rolling of the eyes? In that moment, we have a choice to make. Will we focus on the pain of rejection and give up, or will we realize they need a good example of Who Jesus is, and do our best anyway?

I'm pleased to say that my girl got up under the watchful eye of a couple teammates who stayed to make sure she was okay, and fought through it. She cried the first half mile, running in pain but burning with a competitive fire deep down inside, and finished with all students from the offending school well behind her: third girl, and fourth overall of sixty-plus runners, with a 14.36 two-mile time!

I wish to do so well in every challenging situation I face! God is always with me, like He is with you, like He was with my daughter on the course that afternoon. There are those around us who enjoy knocking us down, or pushing our buttons to see if they can make us blow a gasket, or hitting us in our weak spot to intentionally cause pain. Unfortunately, life isn't a fair game. Fortunately we know the Ultimate Judge, Who sees every shot we take, and rewards people appropriately. Our jobs are to forgive, turn over to Him the responsibility of handling the offenses, take any course of action He lays in our hearts, pray for them, keep it to ourselves; and to hold fast~ not becoming dissuaded from our course by others.

Sometimes I've done well and let Him handle unjust and distracting situations from the beginning. Sometimes I sit and cry, focusing on the injury instead of my Provider/ Defender/ Comforter. Other times I do give it to Him~ but only after I've made a mess of it. Bottom line is: He knows what we deal with: He was here on our planet as a human being. He knows the internal fortitude and personal motivation it takes to overcome the garbage we face, and the spiritual strength that is available with just one word: the Name of Jesus!

My Lord God, thank You for picking me up, dusting me off, and set-

ting me back on my course to run! Regardless of the cost, Father, give me the motivation to continue to grow closer to You; it doesn't matter who approves or disapproves of me, or who cuts in to take me off focus. I give You first place in my heart, and permission to check my motives. I want to run step in step with You!

In Jesus' Name, Amen

Life on the Leash

Ask and it will be given to you; seek and you will find; knock and the door will be opened to you. For everyone who asks receives; he who seeks finds; and to him who knocks, the door will be opened." (Matthew 7:7-8)

he man who enters by the gate is the shepherd of his sheep...the sheep listen to his voice. He calls his own sheep by name and leads them... his sheep follow him because they know his voice." (John 10:3-4)

I like to run, and since getting her, my puppy Freedom has been my constant companion. She's awesome! Now that she's one, she stays with me much better-- not that I'm fast or anything, but we pace together better. She's learned different commands and signals I use when we're out on the road-- she's "tuned in" to me. She knows that it's important we stay together. She knows she's not allowed to run in the fields after the birds. She knows my voice when I say "ok" and pick up the pace. She knows when I say "all done" and we walk. She knows when I say "sit" in the presence of an oncoming car. Her ears perk when I praise her with "good girl" and I can almost see her smile. She often peeks up at me with her big golden eyes, waiting for my next cue as to what's coming as we're trotting along. She also knows that I changed the course we used to take in favor of the one we now run, to keep her away from the angry loose dogs that would run out at us from their hiding spots and cause me to scoop her up quickly in my arms for safety. She trusts me to take good care of her.

One particular day when she was younger, she was fighting the leash, or I suppose more appropriately: fighting my lack of speed with her on the leash. Tugs on the leash to her choke collar didn't work. Speaking to her didn't get her attention. Finally I stopped, and she gasped for air as she kept straining forward, until she gave up and obeyed my command to sit down. I talked to her, Mom to pup, as I rubbed her ear, and told her how much easier it was if we walked together. I knew where we were going, and what pace we would use to get there. "It's a lot easier on you if you stay in step with me," I assured her.

We resumed our trek down the road, and about that time I heard from above "You know, sometimes I feel the same way" from my heavenly Father. Ouch. Yet how true!

How often do I push and strain to get ahead, excited or anxious to see what's around the corner? How often do I form my own plans and try to chase the birds in the field instead of "staying in step" with the One Who knows my course, and the pace I truly can handle?

There have been times when God has "yanked my chain" for running ahead, or in the wrong direction-- not because He doesn't love me, but because He does! His desire is for me to pace correctly so as to have the stamina to finish strong.

There have been times I've wished He would change the course. There have been times when I heard the "dogs barking" and saw them running at me, teeth barred, from an unexpected direction-- tragedy struck, but He was there to scoop me up in His strong, ever-capable, loving arms, and hold me safely until my pounding heart steadied again, and my limp muscles regained strength. Because of my experiences with Him I trust

Him. I know His voice. I know better His expectations and directions even though I don't know what's around the next bend. I'm learning to "quit chasing the birds", and not strain so hard for what's next, but to enjoy the time as we walk along the path of life.

I'm getting better at these things through several means. First is Bible reading: He gave us His Word because it's important for us to know His expectations, and the large scope of His plan. Second is prayer and worship. I praise Him and pour out my heart to Him and He meets me in heart-to-heart communication in a special way. Thirdly is books and other people, whether in church or out. God definitely uses these means to reinforce what He teaches me in His Word-- nothing ever takes the Bible's place, but He uses those around me for fresh understanding and confirmation of the lesson(s) I'm learning.

So how about you? How well do you know the voice of the One Who created you and knows every detail of the path you're on? If you know His voice and His heart, well~ great!! Life is an amazing adventure as you "pace" with Him! If you're not so sure, just begin by talking out loud to Him. He will answer in your heart. His promises are true and He is trustworthy: those who seek Him find Him when they seek Him with their whole heart!

FATHER GOD, today I choose to seek You, not half-heartedly, but with my whole being. I choose to walk in step with You, in the plan You have selected for my life. Thank You for Your faithfulness, that I know I will find You, and know You deeper each step of the way.

In Jesus' Name, Amen

Knowing God's Will

..but the people who know their God will firmly resist him. (Daniel 32b)

*For this reason also, since the day we heard of it, we have not ceased
to pray for you and to ask that you may be filled with the knowledge of His will in all spiritual wisdom and understanding, so that
you may walk in a manner worthy of the Lord, to please Him in
all respects, bearing fruit in every good work and increasing in the
knowledge of God; strengthened with all power, according to His glorious might, for the attaining of all steadfastness and patience; joy-
ously giving thanks to the Father, Who has qualified us to share
in the inheritance of the saints in light. (Colossians 1:9-12)*

Do you ever doubt that you can know God's will for your life, or
think He has it hidden so only the "super spiritual" among us could ever
know it? Well, above we have two verses, one from the Old Testament
and one from the New, that state otherwise! Whew! The purpose for our
life doesn't have to be mystery! Not only does He want us to know our
destiny and His will, but He expects us to have such a relationship with
Him that, as we see in the first reference, we also know who to resist
because he is contrary to His will. In the first verse, the people who know

God are resisting the anti-Christ. At first it may sound like that should be a simple thing to do, but a passage in the book of Revelation states he will be so crafty and subtle in some areas that even the elect would be led away if that were possible. Hmmmm, sounds like a good idea to get to know Him well now, before that time comes, so we're not at risk and easily led away, but solid in our relationship with our Creator.

The second passage contains some great words I really like: pleasing Him, full of knowledge, bearing fruit, power, giving thanks, sharing in the inheritance~ great things to look forward to!

Where does it all start? In our daily decision to spend time with Him and consult with Him on different choices we face. It's about not doing all the talking in our "God time" but taking time to listen as well~ it's supposed to be a dialogue conversation~ not a monologue! Friendship is a two-way street. Think of hanging out with your best friend: there are times one of you needs to talk on a serious level because of what's going on in life, but there are also times you can just hang out in silence, or your back-and-forth banter is punctuated with laughter. There are times you laugh, cry, vent, and there are probably times you have to address a misunderstanding to smooth things out, too.

As God takes us through times like this and we develop the trust in Him that He's always there to see us through, our knowledge of Who He is increases. As this develops, so does the internal feeling that compels us to share what we know of Who He is with someone else in need, and thus we bear fruit and praise Him for it. In His Word is our power. It is life itself! Is it too much to spend fifteen minutes a day to develop a deeper relationship with the One Who knows why we were created in the first place? His will is not hidden, but neither is it microwave- instant. It's more like a flavorful spice blend that has simmered over time. The explosion on your taste buds as the complexity unfolds in your mouth is something you have to experience yourself!

Father God, I want to know You. I commit to tell You about decisions I need to make, either major crossroads or mundane as they may be right now~ I know You want to help me make the most of them. Father, I choose to listen for Your voice, so I may please You, reach my destiny, and enjoy the rewards of a satisfying relationship with You!

In Jesus' Name, Amen

The Irrevocable Call!

He who began a good work in you will carry it on to completion until the day of Jesus Christ. (Philippians 1:6b)

for God's gifts and His call are irrevocable. (Romans 11:29)

Have you ever heard an older person talking with a young college student, lamenting about the career choice s/he made years ago, wishing for the opportunity to go back and do it again, this time choosing to do what they love and not what just paid the most or what parents pressured them into?

Have you seen someone who is living outside of relationship with God yet they have an uncanny ability to sense things? Chances are that part of God's intended gifting for them is to have spiritual sight, and what you are witnessing is that same gift limited in operation by human understanding and enemy counterfeiting. How much more satisfying it would be for that person to operate in the fullness of their gift!

Have you seen someone in a top business position who makes leading an organization look easy yet s/he tells you s/he feels unsatisfied and restless on the inside? It may be that God's plan for that person really is in the leadership arena, but with human effort alone s/he is incorrectly planted.

The leadership gift won't rise to its full potential and the person won't find satisfaction until the gift is reconnected with the Giver of the gift.

Perhaps you see yourself in one of those categories. I think at times most of us have either "been there" or come very close to it. The good news is that even though we detoured and haven't followed His plan exactly up to this point, we can never mess up life so badly that we thoroughly disqualify ourselves, despite the missed opportunities in the past! We can't go back and make the most of those moments, but we can dig in to learn to apply His gifting inside us for the next opportune time~ I guarantee you it will come! Being correctly planted, and connecting the gift back to the Giver brings satisfaction, joy and peace to our hearts.

So have you taken inventory of yourself? Do you know your gifting and occupational calling? When do you most feel an internal sense of peace and fulfillment? Chances are it's those times when you are working within your God-given gifting~ so go develop it! Holy Spirit will empower you to get on track and then flow as you tune in to Him and follow through with each step of reaching your destiny. He will always back you up as you step out in faith!

Has a project at work reached a stand-still with the person assigned to it, but God gave you the next three steps of how to chart the course? Take it upline for approval. Do you see someone hurting or in need, and God drops into your heart the exact words s/he needs to hear?? Don't just wonder where it came from and walk by~ answer the tugging and step into the next level of destiny fulfillment.

Be obedient to God! He will always back you up! His call is in your heart!

Father God, thank You for not giving up on me despite my human failings. Thank You for working on me until I'm complete. Thank You that You don't take away my gifts or destiny, but those are here to stay! Work on my heart, so I can better use these deposits from You in the sphere of influence around me, to bring glory to Your Name,

In Jesus' Name, Amen

Righteous, Not Condemned

God made Him Who knew no sin to be sin for us, so that in Him we might become the righteousness of God. (2 Corinthians 5:21)

and be found in him, not having a righteousness of my own that comes from the law, but that which is through faith in Christ- the righteousness that comes from God and is by faith. (Philippians 3:9)

There is therefore now no condemnation to those who are in Christ Jesus, because through Christ Jesus the law of the Spirit of Life set me free from the law of sin and death. (Romans 8:1)

What does God see when He looks at me? Once I have received His Gift of Jesus as my Savior He sees me as righteous! He sees me righteous like Jesus! How cool is that! My spirit was saved; my spirit cannot sin anymore. My spirit doesn't struggle~ all that struggle comes from my mind, will and emotions that also reside in the "earth suit" of my physical body.

Don't get me wrong now: I am responsible for what my body does and what my mind thinks, but God knows those two parts of me are being renewed and transformed by my time with Him and in His Word.

My spirit is righteous even when I commit a sin. Depending on your religious background, this can be quite the concept to get your head around, can't it?

Think of it like this: when my kids mess up, I don't kick them out of the house, change their last name legally and deny they are part of my family, do I? Nor do I change it again when they do something I like and bring them back home; that would be silly! If I as a human parent wouldn't treat my children in such an irresponsible manner, why would I think the Perfect, Unconditionally Loving Father would do that to me? My name is in His Family Book of Life. The more time I spend with Him, the more you can see the "family resemblance".

Don't waste your time feeling unworthy to approach the throne of grace to receive what you need! Don't fall prey to the lie that you must serve some kind of penance and spend an undefined time "in the dog-house" before you can return to Him. The Bible is Good News that we don't have to try to be righteous in and of ourselves and our works, but our righteousness comes through faith in Him! Because of forgiveness we do not stand before Him condemned, but clean and pure. Read it for yourself: it's not "too good to be true"~ it is the Truth!

Precious Father, expand my mind to receive Your Truth of my righteousness in Jesus . You wrote it in black and white so I can read it for myself! My self image and our relationship transform as I see myself through Your eyes. Thank You!

In Jesus' Name, Amen

Full-Spectrum Colors of Promise

The heavens declare the glory of God! (Psalm 19:1)

And God said, "This is the sign of the covenant I am making between me and you...a covenant for all generations... I have set My rainbow in the clouds." (Genesis 9:12-13)

There is a season for everything under heaven. (Ecclesiastes 3:1)

This morning the sky was dark with the signs of seasonal change, you know~ the dark blue-purple of a sky heavy with rain-turning-to- snow. As we dropped our youngest daughter off at school, God thrilled us by parting the clouds and causing sunshine refraction through the rain, creating a rainbow! Now, that's a nice way to send her in for a day of school~ gazing up at the sign of God's love for her!

As I jogged the last stretch of the distance home with my puppy, He sent another one; this time it was for me: brilliant full-spectrum color against the threat of inclement weather, lighting up the sky around me. His promise was given in Noah's day, yet still holds true for me and you today.

What a God! We live in such uncertainty in our times: politics, the health industry upheaval, employment~ or lack of it, on and on. And through it all, God's promise of love continues, high above. Unhindered. Unshakable. Unending. His promises~ all of them~ endure! His love for you~ yes, you personally, completely unconditional, written in the sky for all to see, assuring you He remembers...

Dear Heavenly Father, thank You for Your steadiness and steadfastness, for Your unchanging love that I can trust in uncertain and ever-changing times! The heavens declare Your glory, and so will I!

In Jesus' Name, Amen

Vote with God

I urge then, first of all, that requests, prayers and interces-
sion and thanksgiving be made for everyone- for kings and
all those in authority, that we may live peaceful and quiet
lives in all godliness and holiness. (1 Timothy 2:1)

Did you vote yet? I did. I see it as my God-given responsibility, as well as my civic duty in the Land of the Free and the Home of the Brave. It's a right, a responsibility, and a privilege. I have been praying for our country and over this election for an extended period of time, as have many Christians around the land. The stakes are high~ higher than I've ever seen them. We are urged strongly by the Apostle (visionary leader of the Church) Paul to pray for them all. In his day they didn't have the freedom and opportunity to vote, but nothing could stop or block their prayers! Living in the midst of an occupied land, they were not powerless or hopeless once they tapped into their Source of Strength and Power! If first-century Christians can have hope, how much more can we! If they can influence their leaders with the political handicap of no representative voice, how much more can we??

Don't limit yourself to what your eyes see, to the physical realm! Remember Elisha and his servant the day they were surrounded by the soldiers of Aram? The servant was afraid because of what he saw with his eyes. Elisha saw with his spirit, and boldly declared "Don't be afraid... those who are with us are more than those who are with them." And Elisha prayed, "Oh Lord, open his eyes so he may see." Then the Lord opened the servant's eyes, and he looked and saw the hills full of horses and chariots of fire all around Elisha." 2 Kings 6:16-17.

What do you see when you look around? Do you see God interacting in the physical realm to make your faith declarations a reality? Or do you only see in one dimension: the fear and despair of this world? Also remember, that God is watching over His Word to perform it! God declared that His Word will not return to Him void, and He is watching to see it fulfilled! (Jeremiah 1:12) Is His Word coming out of your mouth? What does God hear you saying? Is that what you want Him to do?? If not, change what you're saying and make it line up with His Word! Say Jeremiah 32:17 "Ah, Sovereign Lord, You have made the heavens and the earth by Your great power and outstretched arm. Nothing is too hard for You!" Get big and bold on the inside and say God's Word back to Him. Declare "My God reigns!" Declare "no weapon formed against (me or my country) will prosper, and (we) will refute every tongue that rises against (us)", Isaiah 54:17. Pray to God for our leaders to see Him as He is, for supernatural wisdom to lead and decide. Do this with a repentant heart fully dependent on Him~ for every step taken, and every breath we draw...

Father God, I pray Your covering over our land. I pray Your hand on our leaders and those being elected today. May we as a people hear You in our hearts and not harden ourselves against You but work with You to vote in a way that pleases You. Psalm 68:1 "May God arise, may His enemies be scattered!"

Lord, have mercy on us and heal our land as we turn back to
You, fully. Cover us with Your feathers, hide us in Your hand,

and may our leaders stand for You and Your Word in a way that is unprecedented in our history! Father God, hear us and perform a work in our land that will restore us to the great country You have intended us to be since our inception.

In Jesus' Name, AMEN!

Replenish

May the peace of God rule in your hearts. (Colossians 3:15)

We have just entered a season called Advent, which is the preparation time before Christmas. No, it has nothing to do with Black Friday or Cyber Monday, either... It is actually is about getting our hearts ready to celebrate the greatest Gift ever given. Our society places high value on "getting that special gift for everyone on your list", but in the hustle and bustle, often overlooks not only the best Gift ever given, but also the rest of the values and qualities that go along with this season, which make it wonderful in our hearts, not just looks.

In an effort to have an organized and welcoming home for your soon-to-arrive guests, have you felt your stress level rise and snap at your kids, who are goofing around instead of helping you clean? In an effort to give that special gift for everyone, have you spent every available moment shopping, and lost the family balance? Do you find yourself "just making it" to the Christmas holiday on your last burst of energy, only to feel a hollow disappointment as the kids are grumpy, your spouse feels distant, and you just want to curl up on the couch for a while?

Where did it all go wrong? The house looks like the Hallmark commercials, it smells like Rachel Ray has visited, but it feels more like the cold cave of the Abominable Snowman than the Thomas Kinkade come-to-life you intended!

Do you want this year to be different? It can be! The reason to celebrate this season is Jesus. When our motives in giving are out of love and gratitude for the one who receives instead of "keeping up with the Jones' ", we take off the unnecessary pressure and mirror the Ultimate Gift-Giver. Qualities that He displays are peace, joy, hope! As we re-focus, taking time to read our Bible~ God's Word to us, and pray~ talking with God, our hearts will be changed, our vision cleared, and peace, hope and joy replenished.

Where will you find the time to add this "something else" on top of your plate? Even five or ten minutes of connection with God can make a big difference! Can you really afford not to??

Father God, You know the chaos that is my schedule this season. I choose to turn to You as I make choices with my time and the gifts I give. May my choices and attitudes mirror Yours as I make the effort to spend time with You. Whether I am deep in my understanding of You, or just starting out on this journey, I trust You will be faithful with whatever investment I make, and together we will see the positive results in my life!

In Jesus name, Amen

Can You See Through the Fog?

*No, in all these things we are more than conquerors through
Him Who loved us. For I am convinced that neither death
nor life, neither angels nor demons, neither the present nor
the future, nor any powers, neither height nor depth, nor anything else in all creation will be able to separate us from the love
of God that is in Christ Jesus our Lord. (Romans 8:37-39)*

We live in a low-lying area, a small town with two nice-sized lakes. This morning dawned a crisp twenty-four degrees~ it felt extra cold after yesterday's forties! Because of the drop in temperature, the water in the lakes was warmer than the air temp, which caused huge billowing clouds of steam to rise off the lakes and drift ashore, coating every blade of grass and leaf on the landscape with a heavy layer of frost that glimmered with each ray of sun able to pierce through the fog.

Ahhh, the sun! It was there, for sure, causing me to wear my sunglasses on the drive to school to deliver my precious cargo for the day. It was hazy-bright, diffused through the fog, shadowy in places, blinding in others. The morning radio DJ promised an afternoon of sunshine and warmth, but it was far from that at the moment he predicted it! I knew the sun's warming essence would eventually burn off the fog, warmth winning out over the cold in the misty morning battle, yet for me it couldn't happen fast enough! I wanted to locate the straight, full-on sunshine and let it warm me through and through, until my whole body relaxed and relished in it...but that fog kept getting in my way!

Ever been there in your spiritual life? We know Who the SonShine is. And we know there's a spiritual battle between good and evil that typically we cannot see in the physical realm. On top of that, there's the challenge of keeping our mind, will and emotions in check in the midst of circumstances that fog our vision of the Son, attempting to diffuse His power in our lives.

We can win. He wants us to win. He has equipped us to win. But not everyone does- in fact, sadly most don't. It boils down to this: will we stay in the SonShine~ in the Word of God and prayer, confessing His Truth from our mouths despite visible circumstances, and trust that beyond the fog His light shines clearly, brightly? As we stay in the SonShine, His transforming, healing, empowering love burns away the fog and our vision clears. As we remain, we feel the warmth of His love on our cheek, then enveloping us, warming us through and through until the chill is gone, and He has won, no~ we have won, with Him!

Father God, I need the power of Your Love and Truth to burn off the chill and the fog, and the pain I encounter here. Today I choose to remain in the SonShine, soaking up Your rays and speaking Your words out of my mouth, because despite the circumstances I see, I am a co-heir with Christ, and as I remain in You, together we win!

In Jesus' Name, Amen

Fresh Snow and Open Arms

"Come now, let us reason together" says the Lord. "Though your sins are like scarlet, they shall be as white as snow..." (Isaiah 1:18)

For He (God) made Him (Jesus) Who knew no sin (had never sinned) to be sin for us, that we might become the righteousness of God in Him. (2 Corinthians 5:21)

We recently had a fresh Michigan snowfall~ something that is pretty common up here this time of year, and with the heavy winter it's been, I know more areas of the country can relate to this picture than ever before. The thing that set this day apart, though, was the sunshine~ this time of year that's the piece that is uncommon! The sky was blue~ deep blue. The wind was cold, but the sunshine glistened atop the fresh flakes that had fallen all through the night, now creating the bright illusion of warmth. Looking down at the white layer almost required sunglasses, and more than a little squinting because of the piercing brightness that reflected the sun's rays.

That's as close of a picture as I can get for you of how God sees us when He looks at us. He is holy. He is righteous~ we know that, but us... righteous?? You may be thinking, "Oh, but you don't know what I did this weekend..."

Two questions for you: have you asked Jesus into your heart, which includes asking forgiveness for past sin and putting Him in charge of your life?

Have you, since "the weekend" asked again for forgiveness?

If the answer to those questions is "yes", then it's over!

You are forgiven: clean bright and spotless, like the blinding fresh snow, undisturbed, untainted with mud and dirt and sin. Between you and God, it's like those things never happened; sin gets thrown into His "Sea of Forgetfulness".

You see, the second we ask Jesus to come into our hearts, ask for forgiveness, and make Him not only Savior but Lord, our spirits are clean and bright as that snow! They have not just "been cleaned up" but "made completely new" and restored into right relationship with Him.

Our spirits cannot sin, but our bodies can. Our mind, will and emotions can. They are the parts of us that are in the process of being renewed, regenerated, transformed into His likeness. I know, I've thought it too: why doesn't it work like that with my whole self instead of just my spirit?

I don't have a good answer on that, I just know that God works with us on this. There's no limit to how many times we can come to Him and sincerely say "Hey Dad, I blew it again; I'm sorry, please forgive me" and He does! Again, the second we come and ask forgiveness, those things are gone! When He looks at you, He sees you just as holy, clean and righteous (in right standing with Him) as Jesus is! How 'bout them apples??

So you had a rough weekend; or maybe it's been longer than that since you've approached Him. Don't wait another moment! The enemy of your soul is the one who wants to keep you in the lie of "You've apologized and asked forgiveness soooo many times He's tired of hearing from you! You? Back again?? With the same issue?? No way..." That, my friends, is called condemnation. It's not from God: Father, Son or Holy Spirit! It's a lie to keep you separated from Him, the One Who knows your destiny, the One Who loves you so incredibly much He gave His Son's life for your own, in trade for you! Shut your ears to enemy lies and run to your Dad~ whether it's the first time or the billionth time. His arms are open to you; His love is limitless!

Dad, Thanks for keeping Your arms open to me. Thanks for making me shine as white and brilliant as the fresh fallen snow when I let You wash away the sin, renewing a right spirit within me! Please forgive me for.....

Thank You,

In Jesus' Name, Amen

Gratitude: the Attitude of the Season!

We always thank God, the Father of our Lord Jesus
Christ, when we pray for you. (Colossians 1:3)

Give thanks to the Lord, for He is good; His
love endures forever. (Psalm 107:1)

I have learned to be content whatever the circumstances. I know
what it is to be in need, and I know what it is to have plenty. I have
learned the secret of being content in every situation, whether well
fed or hungry, whether living in plenty or in want. I can do every-
thing through Him Who gives me strength. (Philippians 4:11b-13)

When was the last time a series of TV commercials came on, telling
you what you "need" to be happy, and instead of getting frustrated about
the things you aren't choosing to or can't provide for your family, you
turned the volume down and had the family list things they are thankful
for? Our human nature is insatiable, and marketing geniuses know how to
use this. Of course there are things we need~ God knows that. But current
American mind-set is that gratification of a desire should be instant, and

all desire and meaning in life can be satiated from a material standpoint.

Paul, the writer of both the first and third verses above, knew the extremes of human condition. He knew what it was to be "a Hebrew of Hebrews", touted at the top of Jewish society, with every indulgence allowed. He also knew the rank conditions of Roman prisons, chained, standing somewhere between ankle- and waist-deep in sewage, with none of the privileges of American prisons, for years at a time. Yet despite desperate conditions, he was grateful and thankful, and repeatedly stated this! His salvation, freedom and relationship with Jesus gave him revelation and comfort. They were his source of strength to be grateful despite physical conditions. His mind-set was on things above, where his Jesus and his treasure were.

Wow, what a lesson! I know I have numerous reasons to be thankful this Thanksgiving week, and I'm sure you do too. I have three beautiful, healthy, sweet girls. I have great parents who love and support us in our goals. I have a relationship with my Living Lord, Who reveals Himself to me daily. Having been healed from asthma, I have a perspective that God holds my every breath~ I don't take something that simple for granted, but know that without Him I am nothing and can do nothing. I have a warm home and food to eat and two adorable puppies....

How's your list? Of course there will still be things you want~ trust me: my kids can come up with quite the "wish list" for Christmas too~ but let's not miss the blessings we have and the opportunity to be grateful for what we do have! Inside each of us is a God-shaped void that nothing else can fill~ but once it is filled, gratefulness flows and both material and spiritual things are put into proper perspective.

Father God, I am so thankful for You! Thank You for filling the void in me and giving me You! Thank You for the blessings of every breath, and the wonderful way my body is made to func-

tion. Thank You that nothing can separate me from Your love! Thank You for the opportunity to share my gratitude with others who may be in short supply of this commodity at the moment~ I know You will keep me supplied and over-flowing as I look to You!

In Jesus' Name, Amen

A Favorite Song

*Give thanks to the Lord, for He is good; His love
endures forever. (1 Chronicles 16:34)*

*Give thanks to the Lord for His love endures for-
ever. (2 Chronicles 20:21b)*

*Give thanks to the Lord for He is good. His love endures forever.
Give thanks to the God of gods, His love endures forever. Give thanks
to the Lord of lords; His love endures forever. Give thanks to the
God of heaven. His love endures forever. - (Psalm 136:1-3, 26)*

"Give thanks to the Lord, our God and King, His love endures forever!"
This line is out of one of our favorite praise and worship songs!

As we prepare to celebrate this Thanksgiving holiday with our loved
ones, it is important to remember that even in this time of economic
distress and hardship that has befallen our country, God's love endures!

When this song played, I thought out loud, "We must thank Him
today for loving us, sending His Son to die for us. Think about that:
would we be willing to sacrifice one of our children for the hope of an

entire world?" It would be a very tough decision for any parent. Here is the awesomeness of our God: He did do it, without hesitation! There was no debate, just His sure decision that we were all worth it; and that is why we come together this weekend. We must "give thanks to the Lord our God and King, His love endures forever, sing praise, sing praise!"

Father God, as we approach this Thanksgiving season, we choose to take time in our celebrations to say Thank You for loving us so much that You chose to send your Son Jesus to die on the cross for our sins and to pay the price so we can spend eternity with You in Heaven.

In Jesus' Name, Amen

The George Bailey Principle

As long as the earth endures, seedtime and har-
vest...will never cease. (Genesis 8:22)

Most of us have heard of this "seedtime and harvest" principle. In its most basic form, it means "you get what you give". This year I saw it in a classic Christmas movie...

A few nights ago, we sat down as a family on the couch and loveseat, snuggled together, and watched It's A Wonderful Life. Our girls are young, and this was their first time seeing it. They were mesmerized, even though it was late night for them. We talked a lot about what was happening, since there were many commercial breaks.

The movie's main character, George Bailey gave, and gave, and gave. He didn't make millions, like his buddy Sam~ but he gave his counsel to Sam, which paved the way for Sam's business success. He wasn't a war hero like his brother Harry~ but he saved Harry's life in a boyhood accident so he could be a hero to others and save their lives when he grew up. He gave his honeymoon money so the people who trusted in him and his company could make it through until the banks opened back up after a bad run. He gave people a chance when they wanted decent housing, even though others thought he was crazy. He gave his heart to Mary and his children, and provided for them the best he could. Not all of George's giving was monetary: along with business venture capital and personal financial loans, George gave trust, loyalty, kindness, friendship, second chances, and hope for a better future. The movie doesn't say George realized the principle of sowing and reaping, but he benefited from it just the same.

At one place in the movie, his lowest point, we see George on the verge of suicide so Mary could collect on his life insurance policy and pay the debt he owed~ he was willing to give up his life to take care of his family, erroneously believing he was worth more dead than alive. This is when the law of sowing and reaping came into play: all those folks into whose lives George had generously sown, repaid him when he needed it most. God provided, using the people around him. The debt was not only paid in full, but in over-abundance: above and beyond what was actually needed!

Not only is this movie a classic in our culture, but it shows an important aspect of God's character and one of His laws in action. The law of sowing and reaping cannot be violated. We will reap what we sow. As the Bible says, God will not be mocked. There's no escaping this, just as there's no escaping gravity! As to God's character, it shows how He cares for us, His kids, we who have accepted the gift of Jesus Christ's payment for our sin to pave the way to God. God cares for us and delights in the prosperity of His kids! He isn't a God of "scarcely enough." He is a God of super-abundance! He isn't the God of "just barely makin' it." He's the God who said "wealth and riches are in the house of the righteous!"

Are you experiencing the abundance of God's grace in your life today? How's your level of sowing? Have you been into His Word enough to know the promises that are waiting for your contemporary life in modern society, or does your Bible collect dust from lack of use because you think it's irrelevant to your situation?

I'm not pointing fingers~ we all have room for improvement, but I am intending to be thought-provoking. If you had a huge need, like George Bailey, have you planted enough seeds of kindness, generosity, loyalty and friendship, along with finances, that God could use the fruit of your investment in others to meet your need?

Father God, I love You, Your Word, and Your promises! Teach me to see others and their needs with Your eyes, and match my resources to meet their need. Give me the courage to touch the life of another in Your Name, to Think Outside mYself (T.O.Y.) and be Jesus to those around me. I trust You to lead me to those who need to see You through me.

In Jesus' Name, Amen

Sloshy Boots

for we do not have a High Priest (Jesus) who is unable to sympathize with our weaknesses but we have one who has been tempted in every way just as we are- yet was without sin. (Hebrews 4:15)

and being in such anguish, He prayed more earnestly, and His sweat was like drops of blood falling to the ground. (Luke 22:44)

This morning on my walk with my puppy it seemed she was dragging me along. I was wearing my daughter's boots, which were a full size too big yet they were the first ones I found since mine had been relocated to an as-yet undisclosed location by an unidentified person... My socks were sliding off my feet, the heavy boots "clumped" with every step. My cheeks, nose and fingers were cold despite the extra layers I wore. The houses and trees along the street we walked faded into the mist in front of me, and from somewhere in the thick, misting gray expanse above, the geese called but I couldn't find them. Passing cars sprayed the warming slop of snow as they sped off to their destinations. With the passing and fading of each one it seemed we were alone in the whole wide world as my steps echoed and the wet fog grew thicker...

"Some people live in a fog like this all the time; this is their reality,"

I thought to myself. Fortunately for me, I knew there was more. The completeness of my reality has little to do with the weather and my life is bigger than what I see and feel, even on the hard days. I knew I had loving children waiting for me at home, and chili in the crock pot for lunch. Its scent was sure to greet me as I opened the front door of my warm home, and my girls welcomed me back with hugs. I knew the sun was above the clouds, always there, despite the fact I couldn't see it at the moment. And I knew Christ resides within me and the concept of being alone had nothing to do with being lonely. Others, however, plod through life believing that what they see is all there is, believing that everyone else feels satisfied, fulfilled and happy while they are alone. This time of year brings out not only the best in people~ a time to be generous and thoughtful, but also the worst, by highlighting lack of purpose and direction, family dysfunction, loneliness and despair. Some folks live their whole lives in that seemingly inescapable gray mist.

The Good News for all of us is this: the Little Baby whose birthday we celebrate this month can identify with them! He left the greatness and perfection of heaven to put on a physical body, come to earth, grow into a man and experience every single emotion we deal with. Why? So we would know He understands and has compassion on each one of us. He knows what it's like to be betrayed by those closest. He knows what it is to grow up poor. He knows what it is to battle inside His soul. He knows what it is to be totally and utterly alone in the entire universe.

In Gethsemane, His favorite garden, He was betrayed by one of His chosen buddies~ His ministry treasurer. He sweat blood during His prayer time as He battled to put down His human emotions and submit Himself perfectly to God and the awful death He knew was coming next. He didn't cut Himself to bleed, as people do in our society today, but internally He faced such agony between crucifixion and restoration for you and me to the Father that He sweat blood. Now that's intense! Not only did He carry your sin and mine when He got to the cross that next night, but He actually became sin for us. His Father, for the first time in the eternity of existence, turned His back on Jesus in that process. Totally, utterly alone. No one to turn to. Nowhere to go. Stripped naked. Hung up for all to see. A huge crowd mocking, laughing, spitting at His fate. And He died in worldly shame. He figured you were worth it~ all of it.

Does He know and understand the challenges in your gray mist today, during this season where the obstacles you face intensify as they close in around you? You bet He does! And He won't just leave you there to struggle alone, either. His desire is to be the Best Friend you've ever imagined, to give you a strength you've never known on your own, and to fill you with strategies that overcome obstacles. His ultimate desire is first your restoration, then the fulfillment of your destiny!

Father God, I know there's got to be more to life than just this gray mist I'm walking around in today. I don't know how, but I hear You understand where I'm at, so here's my junk. Please let this message of hope be real; show me how this restoration and "full life thing" works.

In Jesus' Name, Amen

The Legacy

Train up a child in the way he should go, and when he
is old he will not depart from it. (Proverbs 22:7)

When Samuel grew old, he appointed his sons as judges in Israel...But
his sons did not walk in his ways. They turned aside after dishonest
gain and accepted bribes and perverted justice. So all the elders of Israel
gathered together and came to Samuel at Ramah. They said to him "You
are old, and your sons do not walk in your ways..." (I Samuel 8:1-5a)

Samuel was one of the great prophets of God who led the people of Israel. From his miraculous birth to a barren woman in answer to her deep heart cry to God, he was dedicated to God, even living in the Temple with the priests from approximately age four on. God spoke to him audibly when he was very young- possibly age ten, and from that point forward he was "activated" in ministry. He served many decades in the capacity of revealing God's will to the Israelites. One would think if he could lead a nation then he could certainly lead his own family to follow God. Yet when the time came for a successor, the people readily agreed his sons were unfit to lead! Another had to be chosen and anointed to serve God in this capacity.

I read that and my heart ached! Here was a man who vibrantly served God his whole life, yet for some reason did not leave a legacy to God through his own children! What happened? Was he so busy serving that he forgot to be a father and lost his kids? I'm asking when I get to heaven!

As a Mom, and also as a third generation "preacher's kid," I saw anew the importance of my daily investment in each of my young daughters. The lessons God is teaching me are for me personally, yes, and for me to apply in both business and ministry capacities, but also for me as a parent. I bear the responsibility to lay a proper foundation from which to launch my girls into their adult lives, so they can go above and beyond anything I do for Him and fulfill the purpose of their destinies. Now we have the aid of the indwelling of the Holy Spirit to whisper into our hearts as we make decisions too. The more teachable my heart is toward God, the more I can impart to my girls. The more transparently I live my life before them, the stronger the launching pad they will have for whatever direction He leads them.

I have made a commitment as a parent to do everything I can to submit myself and my girls to our Heavenly Father. I am actively training them up in the way of the Lord, living authentically before them, and encouraging them in developing their own relationship with Father God—not a forced commitment to a stale religious body, but a living, interactive relationship with the One Who loves them more than we do. His Word says they will not depart from it as they grow older. His perfect plan is for each of us as parents to partner with Him in raising these precious children, allowing Him to "fill in the gaps" between our abilities and their needs and create an amazing legacy honoring to Him, full of blessings for us all! I choose to take Him at His Word!

Father God, thank You for the opportunity to partner with You in the enormous task of raising these precious children You have entrusted to me! It's bigger than I am, but I know with Your wisdom and You backing me to fill in the gaps of my lack, my children will know You in a wonderful way! I speak blessing over them and me as we partner with You.

In Jesus' Name, Amen

Faithfully Glorious!

If we are faithless He will remain faithful, for He
cannot disown Himself. (2 Timothy 2:13)

One of God's character traits is His faithfulness. He always does what He says He will do. His love for us never changes. He told us He would love us, unconditionally, no matter what. He is faithful even when we are not~ and yet we are to be in the process of becoming more and more like Him. As a popular song by David Crowder says, "He makes everything glorious, so what does that make me?" Well, that makes us in process of becoming more and more glorious, to reflect the character of our Creator!

So do you feel "glorious?" Probably that wasn't the first word off your lips when you met a family member at the coffee pot in the kitchen and answered the query "Hey, how are you this morning?" More importantly than how you feel is the question, "Are you in the process of becoming glorious?" How are you doing at reflecting God's faithfulness~ both up to Him, and out toward those around you? Let's not forget our faithfulness to our own word in there as well. When we give our word, do we mean it? When we say we'll show up for an event, do we? When we promise to keep a confidence, is our word "good as gold?" If we have vowed "for better or worse" do we live it daily?

The good news is: God does! He is faithful to love us, forgive us, be there for us, never leave us, strengthen us, provide for us, protect us, hear us, and He always welcomes us back with arms wide open when we come running home. He is faithful even when we fall short. His faithfulness to us is truly glorious! He models with us what He desires our level of faithfulness with others to be.

Receive His faithfulness~ don't shrug it off as though you are unworthy of it! Ask for His strength in your inner being to become more faithful with your words and actions. Accept the transforming process of becoming glorious as He is, with faithfulness as one wonderful component.

Faithful Father God, I see the high calling of becoming more like You. Thank You for Your faithfulness to me! I receive it, and ask for Your work in my life to transform me into a glorious child of Yours, faithful in my verbal commitments and the actions that follow. May I reflect You!

In Jesus' Name, Amen

Acknowledgements

There are so many of you who have impacted my spiritual growth and development! Some of you touched my life for only a very brief season, while with others I've been in relationship for years!

Thank you to: my precious girls~ your love and support and belief in me makes my eyes leak happy tears! I love you more than words can say, and thank you for your willingness to step up and help take care of home responsibilities so I could write. To my parents Rev. Richard and Jane Wilson~ for life and leading me to Christ. To Joe and Jo Glover~ God showed me my first miracle through you. To Ron Martoia~ I learned to worship and put on the armor. To Richard Shipp~ God began to unleash what's inside me as you demonstrated spiritual authority and began to train me. To Jon Mark Hott~ for the hours on the phone: explaining, praying, supporting and teaching me how to use the armor. To Pastor Jess and Paula Gibson~ for blessing my home, investing in me and my team, and stepping in as a spiritual leader to our first business. To Beth and Jeff Jones~ for providing the opportunity to be filled with Holy Spirit. To Pastor Ron and Kathy DeGraw~ for further authority training. To my dear sister-in-law Carla~ for your overcoming faith and probing questions which keep me going deeper. To Israel~ for speaking God's clarity into my transition. To Pastor Chapman~ for confirming that word and continuing with us in friendship. To Apostle Barbara Yoder~ for preaching the Breaker Anointing, and calling heaven to earth. To Apostle Chuck Pierce~ for consistently bringing God's fresh word to life, at "just the right moment" in my life. To Pastor Jerry Dirmann~ for The Rock vision, leadership and consistency. To Pastor Neil and Christy Kelly~ for your friendship, guidance, and bringing The Word. To Jeff and Christina Osborn~ for years of armor-bearing in obedience to God's word to you; I thank Him for the call on your life! To Brad Bandemer, for hours of counseling & faithfully teaching me to hear Abba's voice clearly! And most of all thank You God, for life, breathe, the gift of Jesus, my healings, and the opportunity to share You!

About The Author

Robyn's background of schooling in social work, parenting, networking leadership, convention ministry and growing up as a "preacher's kid" give her a unique platform of experience. Her passion is for people to understand the deep love God has for them, and the interactions by which He reveals Himself in everyday life.

Today Robyn resides in southwest Michigan. She is a single Mom of three beautiful daughters and two "fuzzy children", her dogs. After a significant life change she is "thrilled to be able to write again!" and looks toward the future with great anticipation. From parenting to partnering, leadership to worship, her heart will be visible in all the pages she pens.

For more information, visit her at Real Life with a Real God Facebook group, or www.RealLifewithaRealGod.com